BLACK HELICOPTERS II

THE END GAME STRATEGY

Also by Jim Keith:

The Gemstone File
Secret and Suppressed
Casebook on Alternative 3
Black Helicopters Over America
OKBomb! Conspiracy and Cover-up
The Octopus (with Kenn Thomas)
Casebook on the Men in Black

BLACK HELICOPTERS II

THE END GAME STRATEGY

JIM KEITH

IllumiNet
PRESS

Library of Congress Cataloging in Publication Data

Keith, Jim, 1949—
  Black Helicopters II: The Endgame Strategy / Jim Keith
    p.   cm.
  ISBN: 1-881532-14-3 : $14.95
  1.   United States — Politics and government — 1989-
  2.   Conspiracies — United States — History — 20th Century.
  3.   Democracy — United States.
  4.   World politics — 1989-   I. Title
E839.5.K45   1997
322.4'2'0973—dc20

                                                     94-23888

IllumiNet Press
P.O. Box 2808
Lilburn, GA 30048

10 9 8 7 6 5 4 3 2 1

Printed in the United States of America

For the George and Kristin Pickard family

With sincere thanks to my family, Ron and Nancy Bonds, George Eaton and the *Patriot Report,* Hawthorne Abendsen, Terry Romine, Robert A. Luca, Jeff Thompson, Jerry Smith, the Ron and Jan Brown family, Stan Lusak, Eugene Austin, Stephen Volk, Ron Keith, Adam Parfrey and Feral House, Florence Signalness, Mark Greene, Paul Larson, Frederick V. Blahut and Tony Blizzard of *The Spotlight,* David Hatcher Childress and Adventures Unlimited, Harold R. Green, Jr., Wayne Henderson, David Alexander, Tim Cridland, Kenn Thomas and *Steamshovel Press,* R. Seth Friendman and *Factsheet Five,* many friends in the U.S. military and military reserves, both active and retired, who must remain anonymous, and those who helped whose names have been accidentally omitted. Without your assistance this book would never have come into being.

The author welcomes correspondence and information on the topics mentioned in this book. Please enclose an SASE if you would like a reply.

"Today Americans would be outraged if U.N. troops entered Los Angeles to restore order; tomorrow they will be grateful! This is especially true if they were told there was an outside threat from beyond, whether real or promulgated, that threatened our very existence. It is then that all peoples of the world will pledge with world leaders to deliver them from this evil. The one thing every man fears is the unknown. When presented with this scenario, individual rights will be willingly relinquished for the guarantee of their well being granted to them by their world government."

— Henry Kissinger
in an address to the Bilderberg group at Evian, France
May 21, 1992

CONTENTS

INTRODUCTION

BLACK CHOPPERS AND BLACK PR

B lack armored insectoids descend in swarms upon America. Some are fitted with antennae and metallic eyes for surveillance, while others bristle with weaponry, ready to transform an American neighborhood into a surrogate of hell in a second. Around the country these dark marauders storm the sky, and ordinary citizens wonder whether they are harbingers of the end.

These are the mysterious black, unmarked helicopters, seen in virtually every region of the United States since the late 1960s. They have harassed and horrified people, shot at them with bullets and missiles, sprayed unknown chemicals on populated areas, resulting in the death of livestock and people, and have too often been seen in the vicinity of cattle mutilations, secret troop movements, and terrorist attacks.

Once used as a vehicle of military utility, now the helicopter is the aircraft of choice in surveillance, harassment, and the bullying of American citizens who dare speak out about the excesses of a government gone increasingly mad.

Recently, a well known radio conspiracy talk show host suddenly turned completely apolitical when a black chopper ominously hovered a few feet over his rural home during his broadcast. Now all the man will talk about is space aliens, comets, and people who channel Nostradamus in lousy French accents. It doesn't take a Nostradamus to understand his sudden change in program format.

Another radio commentator, operating out of the southern states, Ron Hunter, had the roof of his house strafed by machine gun bullets from a black chopper. Hunter had apparently been too vocal about black helicopters and the New World Order.

When queried about the black choppers, military and aviation authorities disavow any knowledge of what is going on. Usually they shrug or make a crack about rampant paranoia in America, taking their cue from rightwing spokesmodels like Rush Limbaugh, who insists the choppers don't exist.

Some are careful to point out that most military helicopters have been painted in a deep olive drab that appears black from a distance, and that their insignia are so faint as to be identifiable only when seen up close. These OD rigs are paraded out at airshows to prove that the black choppers have a mundane explanation.

So that is the answer, the black helicopters are simply a case of mistaken identity. The military is only doing its duty, all choppers are green, and everything is right with the world.

The experts find it more difficult to explain how, if that is the case, the black helicopters have been out in force and doing their dirty work since the late 1960s, since the military only switched to the OD paint job in the 1990s. They also find it difficult to explain high resolution color photos that show black choppers, not green.

In the community of UFO researchers, they believe they have the inside scoop on the black choppers: they are piloted by extraterrestrials, and fly about the American landscape in shape-shifting flying saucers masquerading as whirlybirds. Might this be what the owners of the black choppers would prefer that we imagine, that they are from outer space?

Although hundreds of hours of heated debate and endless inches of printed copy have been devoted to the phenomenon of the black helicopters on talk radio and in midget-circulation underground newsletters, the national media inexplicably has given short shrift to the subject over the last 25 years. That situation may be turning around.

In March of 1997 the *Strange Universe* television show presented a slightly unbalanced evaluation of the topic, the basic theme being that people who believe in black helicopters are probably paranoid. I was interviewed, and although many of the remarks I made were cut from the presentation when it aired, at least my comments were not butchered into incomprehensibility as has happened before. I had my say, although not precisely all of it, in the minute or so I had to speak.

I had the feeling that the people at *Strange Universe* aired all they felt they could get away with — leaving out, in particular, some choice remarks I made about connections between the choppers, the CIA, and cattle mutilations — but that they were sympathetic to the truth. They knew, however, that there was a wide black line that should not be crossed.

This TV presentation was noteworthy for a side trip the production crew and I took to an Air Force base not far from my home. Using a 30X telephoto lens, the cameraman was able to obtain shots of three black choppers parked on the landing strip, and this footage was shown on the broadcast. I am told by sources at the air base (who must remain anonymous) that after the television show aired, an internal investigation was launched into leaks and "public perception" of the black choppers.

Another televised treatment of the black helicopters was viewed by millions, both on the MSNBC cable news network in April of 1997, and aired again on NBC a few days later. Predictably, this was a slice-and-dice job worthy of Freddy Krueger, condemning everyone who believes in, or has had an encounter with the black choppers, as being a lunatic, a conspiracy freak, and if it had only happened a couple of weeks earlier, probably a member of the Heaven's Gate suicide club.

The majority of my interview with MSNBC/NBC was conducted by an aging media flak with a little mustache, who barely let me answer the questions he posed before interrupting and moving on to the next question. Not an unfamiliar ploy, (actually, it is dubbed the "Rapid Fire Approach" in the Army's Intelligence Interrogation manual, FM 34-52, Appendix H) but one more suitable to secret police bullyboys than to "journalists." Perhaps there is a fine shading between the professions these days.

The fun didn't end with the filming. The interview was hacked into tiny bits in the editing room, and I was not allowed to complete a thought, while what I did say was doled out between snotty little comments inserted later by the same establishment nebbish.

Interviews with two black helicopter witnesses, one who had examined a chopper at close range, and another whose ranch had been sprayed by a chopper, resulting in the death of animals on the property, were filmed at length but not included in the program. There are, after all, no black choppers anywhere, anyhow, thus why mislead the public with the truth?

They even had a squirrely shrinkozoid on the program to psychoanalyze me, without the benefit of ever having met me, or of having read my book. Naturally he pronounced me and anyone who is concerned about the choppers as being a bit wonky. Maybe the shrink had read about that popular if devastating new psychiatric disorder dubbed "government phobia," that was announced in the *Clinical Psychiatry News* of October, 1994. That publication informs us that the phobia is "characterized by a persistent fear, despite any facts to the contrary, of all governmental agencies." People who suffer from the complaint "develop tightness of the chest, palpitations, diaphoresis, and several other somatic symptoms if they sense any threat that the involvement of the government is increasing around them."

I confess I did experience symptoms of diaphoresis when watching NBC's hatchet job on the black helicopters — that is the technical term for a pain in the neck, isn't it?

My treatment by MSNBC/NBC wasn't a big surprise. I know where that network is coming from, as I assume a good portion of my readership does. Even the establishment media has repeatedly called into question their standards of journalism and faking of news stories. Specifics? Try the *New York Times,* June 21, 1994, page 22; the *New York Times,* June 25, 1994, page 8; and *Time* magazine, March 15, 1993.

Get who NBC is: It interlocks in its directorship with the Federal Reserve, the Rockefeller Foundation, Kuhn, Loeb Co., First City Bancorp, Northrup defense contractors, the Institute of Strategic Studies in London, Atlantic Richfield, Rockefeller Brothers Fund, and a number of companies pivotal in the octopoidal Rothschild/J.P. Morgan banking conglomerate.[1]

Somehow I doubted that either the black choppers or the American public would get a fair shake from this megaphone for globalist fatcats, or from their lackeys with twitchy little mustaches.

NBC, along with all of the other monoliths of American monopo-media, presents a limited bandwidth of information that sidesteps anything challenging to the existing power elite, i.e. the guys in the boardroom who, after all, are just a bunch of good ol' boys who happen to belong to the Trilateral Commission and cavort naked at Bohemian Grove.

I did the interview with NBC anyway since I don't often get a chance to shoot the bull to a million people at once. I knew that a significant portion of the American public would be able to see through whatever sleazy tactics they used to discredit me and the subject of the black helicopters, and that a portion of the message would get through to the perceptive.

By now the better informed among the American public are beyond being deluded by these hired guns of snoresville media and the itchy anal-ists of psychiatry. By now, many Americans have come to doubt every lying, cynical word uttered by the Brokaws and Koppels and Rathers of the world, who, based upon statements of the French government, are mostly in the pay of the CIA, anyway.

A significant portion of the American public has come to pursue enlightenment elsewhere than from the boobs on the boob tube. Proof? Within the last three years evening news broadcasts have lost more than 10 percent of their viewers and, as Robert Lichter of the Center for Media and Public Affairs in Washington tells us, "they haven't the faintest idea what to do about it."

Regardless of "official" pronouncements on the subject and what the almighty dinosaurs of NBC want us to think, the black helicopters do exist, and they have engaged in the illegal oppression of the American populace for over 25 years. They are part of a larger conspiratorial scheme, one of dire importance for every person on this planet to understand. I expect that you will be closer to understanding after reading this book.

It just so happens that the answer to the mission of the black helicopters and who is fielding them cannot be whispered on national TV. You can devote thousands of hours to O.J.'s splatterfest, to Jonbenet's pre-pubescent come-ons, or to a pedophilic popstar's similarity to K-Mart ("Little boys trousers half off"), but God help us if we get hip to the fact that the American republic is being ripped apart by the wolves of conspiracy.

To derail the inevitable criticism that a number of black helicopter eyewitness accounts included in this book are anonymous, there was no way of getting around it. I used this approach primarily in the case of military personnel who felt that revealing their names would cause repercussions to their careers. One of my most valued informants, for instance, is a 32-year veteran of the Department of Defense, Air Staff, and the Joint Chiefs of Staff. These anonymous accounts are included because they provide vital information that cannot be acquired through the "usual" channels (like *George* magazine) — but I assure the reader that in each such instance I have verified that the witness is who they say they are. If you have a real problem with the anonymity of some of my informants, disregard those reports. There are no shortage of accounts with full attribution.

Here is most of what I have found out about the subject of black helicopters since the publication of my first book on the subject in 1974. The information in this book may shock and disturb you, but my ultimate purpose is to make you aware of what is really going on in this country, behind the tawdry shadow show of national media. This is a down and dirty update on what is taking place in America at this very moment.

NOTES:

1. Mullins, Eustace. "Who Owns the TV Networks," undated essay in the author's possession.

1

A BLACK CHOPPER CHRONOLOGY

PART II

Here is a listing of recent black helicopter incidents, updated from the previous volume of this series. I have not attempted to list all of the literally thousands of observations of black or unmarked craft that have been reported, opting for significant or informative sightings.

1994

— During the early part of May, in Ontario, Oregon unmarked black helicopters were seen in repeated overflights at an altitude of about 1,500 to 2,000 feet. Sightings of black choppers resumed in late summer, with unmarked Blackhawk and Apache attack helicopters seen in flight. Also observed in the area during this time were trains and numerous trucks carrying up to 80 Bradley Fighting Vehicles at one time. [1]

— On May 23, 1994, at the Big Meadows on the Blue Ridge Parkway, Virginia, a citizen came upon a blocked-off road leading into the Shenandoah National Park. He observed a black chopper coming in for a landing a short distance away, and took photos of the craft. When he asked a park ranger what the black choppers were doing there, the ranger said, "They help us with search and rescue." Asked about the 40mm grenade launcher the "search and rescue" chopper was armed with, and the black uniforms and black hooded helmets the crew of the chopper were wearing, the park ranger became incensed and said, "Get out of here, because they just help us with search and rescue!"[2]

— In late 1994 and early 1995, numerous unmarked black helicopters including one Russian craft were seen in many flights in northern Arizona, particularly in the areas of Camp Verde and Cottonwood. Four black helicopters were also seen landed in a fenced off Forest Service compound, although a spokesman for the Forest Service later denied that there had been any helicopters there at the time. [3]

— From the *Los Angeles Times:* "Droning helicopters kept hundreds of Oxnard, California residents awake Tuesday night as a detachment of Marines from Camp Pendleton practiced urban navigation training over a quiet residential neighborhood. Simulating a terrorist situation, six Marine Corps helicopters hovered and swooped in the vicinity of the Ventura Freeway and Rose Avenue from about 9:00 to 10:30 p.m., frightening and angering nearby residents.

"'It was loud. They weren't very far from my house,' Oxnard resident Janet Heistad said. 'You could hear this glob-glob-glob, glob-glob-glob. It was irritating, to say the least.'

"The two-hour maneuver featured six helicopters — including AH-1 Cobras and UH-1 Hueys and a small Marine unit on foot in the Oxnard area." [4]

— In San Diego in December, 1994, a pilot-in-training and his flight instructor had a close encounter with a black helicopter. Approaching Brown Field for a landing they heard the following radio transmission:

"Brown Tower, this is two black helicopters at the prison [reportedly a local checkpoint]. Request a full stop landing."

According to the account of the pilot-in-training, the black helicopters were given permission to land behind his own plane. As he taxied down the runway the black choppers approached the field, making two circles and stirring up a lot of dust.

The man recalls, "One helicopter, the leader, was an Apache with a Gatling gun mounted under the chin. The second helicopter was similar to a McDonnell 500E and was festooned with antennae and electronic detection gear. The appearance of the formation was that the 500E detected targets and the Apache shot them up (or down), whichever came first." [5]

1995

— What follows is an excerpt from a letter from a retired member of The Joint Chiefs of Staff, to the Attorney General, James Gilmore III, and the Superintendent of State Police, Colonel M. Wayne Huggins, in Virginia.

One of the men involved in the chopper encounter, Sheriff Spence, a short time before had participated in a broadcast of the well-known anti-New World Order Jack McLamb radio show. The letter is printed with the permission of the author. It begins:

I believe the following chilling account of what happened to Sheriff Bill Spence and Captain C.G. Feldman, on February 14th [1995], may be what's necessary to assure me of your undivided attention.

Three days ago, Bill and CG were on their way from the Sheriff's Office to the monthly county supervisor's meeting in the town of Orange. As they drove south, they noticed a helicopter operating in the immediate area, which then disappeared below the visible horizon. Bill continued to drive the four or so miles toward Orange, passing his home neighborhood in the process. As they neared the outskirts of town, they observed a black, unmarked Cobra attack-gunship, hovering just above the elevated terrain, across Route 20 from Waugh Enterprises. Several people, upon hearing the chopper, had come outside, and were watching. Moreover, 'Bud,' a Waugh motorcycle salesman, confirmed that on the 14th, there was in fact, a chopper operating to the immediate front of the business; as noted above.

Bill pulled his official, unmarked car, off the road. He and Captain Feldman then, in full uniform, exited the vehicle, visually observing the hovering aircraft. Then, as I understand it, the Cobra, which, according to Colonel Hinkle of the U.S. Army Staff Aviation Training Directorate - Pentagon, is normally armed with a 20mm 'Gatling' cannon, immediately climbed up to about 100 feet, and assumed the normal, nose-down 'attack attitude.' The Cobra then executed what is best described as an unorthodox, albeit hostile, tactical attack 'engage-and-evade' maneuver. With the cannon/nose aimed at the two officers, the Cobra commenced a series of rapid pirouettes, circling the lawmen, for approximately three revolutions, continually maintaining a 'gun-to-target' lock on the lawmen. The cannon barrels were clearly visible. Upon completing three revolutions, the Cobra flew up over the town, loitering briefly; subsequently egressing the area. (It was later discovered the chopper had sortied from Peter's Mountain FEMA [Federal Emergency Management Agency] base, Cismont, Virginia, in Albemarle County!)

The sheriff, later, upon hearing from his household, was told that just a few minutes prior to the aforementioned evening, a chopper had hovered directly above the family residence, literally vibrating the windows/structure! Both segments of this incident must be considered to have been performed with hostile/intimidating intent! Furthermore, the Cobra, being unmarked, was in violation of FAA/U.S. identification directives, and was most certainly in violation of low altitude operating criteria, i.e. too low to be performing such a complex, and unnecessary, aerial maneuver in such close proximity to personnel/structures on the ground; particularly in a peacetime, continental U.S. environment!

Additionally, Colonel Hinkle, an Army Staff, rotary wing officer, and a certified Cobra gunship pilot, advised that the U.S. Army had never trained him on this particular (controls-coordinated) attack maneuver. Therefore, it appears to be of foreign origin, and is not intrinsic to U.S.-rotary wing, tactical operations doctrine! Moreover, he asked for the 'airframe number,' and a 'date/time' of the incident. Of course these choppers, as you have been previously advised, don't have markings, nor are they U.S.-controlled assets!

— In April of 1995, during an official visit in the U.S. by the Japanese emperor, a clerk observed a black helicopter landing across the street from the Corner Store in Ruckersville, Green County, Virginia. The chopper deployed several black uniformed, masked, armed troops who fanned out running, and formed a defensive perimeter. They were in a defensive position for approximately 30 minutes, then upon a whistled command (a non-U.S. tactical signaling approach, suggesting that these may have been foreign troops) they remounted the chopper and egressed the area. Employment and deployment happened very fast, and the clerk was startled and very scared.

— From the *Chicago Sun Times,* June 13, 1995, in an article titled "Top-Secret Strafing Wakes Whole Suburb":

"The first thing I heard was the helicopters and the explosions," reported an upset Michelle Velenta, a resident of Des Plaines [Illinois]. "Toward midnight. I ran to the window. Explosions. Helicopters flying off north and south. That's when the gunfire started. Kapow, kapow, kapow. Then another helicopter comes swooping in from the north. It came in so low the trees were swaying."

An upset Valenta continued: "We're near the State Police. A lot of us called. Nobody would tell us anything. It went on for nearly an hour. It was terrifying. Can you help us? A call was placed. Many calls were placed. The Des Plaines Police said they never heard of it. Ditto, at first, the Illinois State Police. Then a trooper said, 'It was some sort of SWAT thing. Uh, multi-jurisdictional. But we can't talk about it.'"

When Valenta asked the state trooper who could in fact talk about it, she was told to contact the Department of Defense.

There was slightly more clarification the day after the helicopter incident, in an article titled, "One Suburb Conquered":

'Routine exercise,' the Defense Dept. said.

'There were these unlit helicopters criss-crossing the rooftops and nearly an hour of explosions, like quarry blasting, enough to rattle our windows,' said Ken K—ra of Lemont.

'Mike Ci—nio of Homer Township joined neighbors running into the street. 'I actually thought one of the [oil] refineries was going up,' he said.

'OK. Fun's fun. What is going on?'

'Routine training exercise,' said Mike Sienda of the Defense Dept.

'That's what you said before. This sounds more like Seven Days in June.'

'All right. Here is what I can tell you. It was military training

for the aviation elements from the U.S. Army Special Op Command
HQ at Ft. Bragg.'
'You came nearly 700 miles to invade Des Plaines and Lemont?'
'It was a navigational exercise.'
'With gunfire and explosions.'
'There was some of that, too.' [7]

— Residents of Crockett, Texas were in an uproar over low
fly-overs of their homes and farms by Army Reserve choppers
in the early months of 1995. An Associated Press news release
reported, "About 40 landowners and ranchers attended a town
hall meeting at the Houston County Courthouse to tell the Army
Reserve that its AH-64 Apache helicopters are spooking their
livestock and unnerving their families.

"'We were terrorized,' said Grapeland resident Truman
Tate. 'Now my 9-year-old is scared to death when an aircraft
comes over.'

"The Army apologized for the inconvenience, but said they
must continue the training over Crockett, which is about 100
miles north of Houston... The reservists say that while trying to
avoid populated areas, they're using parts of 11 rural counties
to perform training exercises to prepare pilots for battle.

"[Reserve Captain Joseph] Ingignoli asked startled residents
not to shine spotlights or shoot guns at the helicopters, as some
have done." [8]

— An anonymous letter was posted to the *Patriot Report* in
1995, signed "Texas Prisoner":

> If I didn't see this with my own eyes every night, I would not
> believe it. For over two years you've been reporting black Federal
> Emergency Management Agency copters buzzing like flies — well,
> they are using prison areas (remote areas, close to towns) here at
> least. These copters have some sort of muffler on them because all
> [that you can hear] is the wop, wop, wop of the blades. They are
> extremely active at night. I just got done watching (for the fifth night
> in a row!) these FEMA copters sporting a single blue and a single
> red light, hover up and down, sideways and forward, and land; then
> speed off and circle and come back. The interesting things are 1)
> These areas are on correctional facility property, 2) There is no

military base nearby, and 3) These flat, weeded areas within thick brush that the inmates cleared, have been run flat by asphalt prep construction equipment...

The U.N. white transport planes at the Amarillo airport are for real. I used to be in that prison right next to the airport. One could see all the planes with no real noticeable markings, and a flat white. There are dozens of them, and they have not been moved off the airport — they just sit there ready to go. [9]

— On August 8, 1995 unmarked helicopters were observed flying toward Inola, Oklahoma. Apparently it was a planned exercise by the military. The main street in town was blocked off by police while the helicopters repeatedly landed and then departed. [10]

— On September 9, 1995, the following report was placed on the Internet, describing a sighting of a Russian helicopter:

Glendale, Arizona, 2:35 p.m. local time:
A Mil Mi-24 Hind has just flown over our house, heading around 170, altitude around 2,500 feet. This is the second time this has happened that I know about — earlier in the year two flew over in formation, again on a Saturday, heading 180, but at around 500 feet.

Does anyone know where these are coming from and where they might be going? I remember reading somewhere of an Army base in New Mexico which is 'evaluating' former Soviet helicopters, but I can't remember which one it is — maybe there is a connection?

The local *Arizona Republic* newspaper has reported on several occasions, sightings of 'mysterious black helicopters' operating in the high desert north of Prescott, and extrapolating the flight paths this would certainly fit — but how credible these earlier reports are I don't know.

In each case the helos have definitely been Hinds, in a very dark camouflage and with no visible markings. —Steve F. [11]

— On October 12, apparently in a bid to quell public concern over repeated fly-overs of Ontario, Oregon by black helicopters, an "almost" all-black AH-6 chopper landed on the baseball field of the local high school. The chopper was reportedly armed with "inert" Hellfire missiles, and a 30 mm cannon.

An Ontario resident using the pseudonym "Peter Cochran" reported, "The students (and faculty) who came out to view this Apache attack helicopter had plenty of intelligent questions to ask the crew and two support personnel. I don't think these U.S. Army personnel were expecting such a response from such a young audience."

After asked why the chopper had landed at the school, one student was told, "we have been asked to come here." On further questioning about who had asked them, the warrant officer could not provide an answer. [12]

— In 1995 and 1996 dozens of individuals living near Casper, Wyoming observed low-flying black helicopters, and suffered thousands of dollars of damage as hovering choppers lifted roof shingles and stampeded horses. Noted during the same period were Russian troops visiting in Casper. The Wyoming National Guard, the Federal Aviation Administration, and the governor of Wyoming disavowed knowledge of the choppers, and the governor's chief of staff, Ken Erickson, told the *Wyoming Tribune-Eagle*, "This does bother us a little. The governor would like to know who they are and the nature of their business."

The governor's headaches had not ended when the following report was filed: "15 March, 1996 — Casper, Wyoming: 37 black choppers flying south were followed by citizens in a twin Beech. The citizens were then chased north by two black Apache choppers. The two choppers had ECM (which garbled all air-to-ground communications) and spoofer transmitters (which 'spoofed' the FAA radar). The Governor of Wyoming called the Pentagon." [13]

1996

— On March 1, 1996 two black helicopters, one a Huey, the other a small observation helicopter, unmarked except for a "white patch or spot" on the side of the chopper, were observed flying just outside Madera, California. The witness noted, in correspondence with the author, "I had a pair of binoculars and I study aircraft and know where such markings should be, and the ones this nation uses were not on these choppers." [14]

— "On March 27, 1996, in Culpepper, Virginia, a 'New World Order'-smart deputy police officer, awakened at midnight and hearing a chopper hovering 100 yards away, picked up his gun and went outside. The chopper had no lights on it, and the noise of the rotor was so loud that it was shaking the deputy's house. The chopper pilot, apparently on seeing the gun, turned on the navigation lights on the chopper and egressed the area - immediately!" [15]

— "On April 14, 1996, at 9:30 a.m. in Culpepper, Virginia, a black Huey helicopter buzzed a house at 50 feet, then buzzed the town of Culpepper six times, scaring the populace. This is contrary to FAA regs, which state '1,000 feet minimum for urban overflight.'" [16]

— "On May 25, 1996, near Casper, Wyoming, in torrential rain, two Americans, looking for a suspected 'U.N. landing zone,' followed two low-flying 'dark colored' Huey choppers to what appeared to be a 'pre-determined off-loading zone.' As they approached from a forward quarter of the now-grounded aircraft, they saw 'suitcase-sized cases' being off-loaded into a blue truck. Apparently they were observed in the rain, and two shots were fired at the men, the bullets passing just overhead. The two men returned fire (two shots) and hit the truck, before it rapidly egressed the area." [17]

— In mid-1996, Pittsburgh, Pennsylvania was assaulted in the middle of the night by nine Army helicopters firing guns and setting off explosions. Residents were terrified, and one woman went into labor. Witnesses said that the choppers flew much lower than FAA regulations allow, knocking over things on the ground with the backwash from the rotors.

After 100 angry citizens called the police department, protesting the U.S. Army Special Command exercises, further exercises were called off. A spokesman for the Army, Lt. Col. Ken McGraw, said that similar exercises had been conducted in other cities, including Los Angeles, Dallas, Miami, and Detroit, but that the Army had never received so many complaints before. After all, Col. McGraw protested, the Army had notified police and citizens several HOURS before the mock assault.[18]

— Researcher Chandra Chandler reports on a number of curious occurrences in Southern Colorado in mid-1996. Many unidentified lights and unmarked helicopters, both black and white, were seen in the area. Chandler also notes "a high concentration of military activities" taking place, with frequent military convoys and men in black uniforms without insignia being observed.

Chandler writes, "They have observed a round yellow-orange light moving slowly over the area and have on numerous occasions tried to chase it, but to no avail. We were able to see this light on our visit with the witness. It came on, went out, then came on, flared brightly, then went out again.

"Unmarked helicopters are common, but after complaints to authorities about the craft, they stopped daylight flights."

Chandler reports on one sighting where "the sky was filled with dozens of twinkling lights that we assume were helicopters. It was quiet on the prairie and we could clearly hear the sound of a passenger jet overhead, but there was no sound from the small, low flying lights."

It is noteworthy that numerous radar tracking stations and towers have built in the same area of Colorado, many of them protected by triple rows of barbed wire. Chandler recalls one witness who, while driving, saw something strange going on at a radar station.

The witness "parked behind a large haystack where he could see, but not be seen. The station went dark, even the light on top of the dish went out, then a square beam of red light pierced the night sky. The beam went up at least 14,000 feet according to the witness. The further up the beam went the pinker it got until it just faded out. The witnesses were amazed that the beam was square and stayed that way." Returning to the area the following night, the "radar facility" was now inactive.

Colorado authorities, when contacted, expressed ignorance of what was going on. [19]

— The following is a report from a former Joint Chiefs of Staff intelligence staff member, and is printed here with permission:

> All testimony and 'sources' indicate that the 17 July TWA 747 jetliner was shot down by an air-to-air missile. From experience in Colorado/Wyoming in 1996, it is known that Soviets/foreigners in U.S. Apache attack choppers are operating with 'spoofer' transmitters in their ECM pods; thus the FAA sector radars cannot see the choppers. If the government 'proves' that it was a shoulder-fired missile, attributed to 'terrorists,' all air travel will cease in the U.S.; especially if another airliner goes down in like manner. Actual eyewitness testimony, audible, visible, and technical, all point to a missile having hit the plane. The possibility of a small heat-seeking, shoulder-fired missile is out of the question. The FAA 'radar blip' could not have been such a small SAM missile. The AF C-130 (Lieutenant Colonel/Major Myers) pilot saw it streaking laterally, not climbing from the ground, towards the TWA 741...
>
> Let's get the press off the 'portable shoulder-fired missile' or 'friendly fire' propaganda. This was a chopper airborne-launch...

The same source reports that on September 30, "A retired Navy admiral was heard complaining at a gun show that the missile that hit TWA 800 was a high-tech, American designed-and-made 'plastic component' weapon. It had to be a continuous rod warheaded missile from the signature of the destruction. It is made of polycarbonate plastics (except the rod) and laminates. He was highly upset about us giving the missile to the foreign multi-national forces which are in the country."

This informant's reports are given additional weight by an internal CBS memo stating that the news department of that network had determined that Assistant FBI Director James K. Kallstrom, in charge of the investigation of the crash, is "convinced it's a missile [that downed flight 800] and that he thinks the Pentagon is withholding information."

The following anonymous letter was faxed to me on August 31, 1996:

I witnessed the crash of TWA flight 800.

I work in a county office in California. My wife and I were on vacation in New York. We were on the beach when it happened. We talked to many other witnesses who saw the same thing we did. A very bright fiery light heading upward toward the jet. Then an explosion.

We told what we had seen to some investigators. We told them that we were on our vacation and about to continue on to Florida. They asked us to stay a while longer and said that they would pay our hotel bill until our statements as to what we saw could be taken by other investigators. We agreed.

It turned out however to be more than just our statements taken. They took our social security numbers, driver license and license plate numbers. They wanted to know my place of employment and the names and addresses of our children and relatives. They questioned us in separate rooms and made us feel like criminals. They said that what we must have seen was a shooting star or some fireworks being shot from the boat. I told them that it was not anything like that at all. I said that it was definitely a flare type rocket heading toward the aircraft when it exploded.

It was then suggested that we did not see anything at all and that we were going along with what other people said they saw, just for the excitement of it. I told them, 'No way, I know what I saw.'

After the questioning we were asked to go back to the hotel and stay there until we were cleared to leave. About three hours later two other men we had not seen before came to the hotel. They gave us some money and told us 'never to mention anything to anyone about being witnesses to the crash again.'

They scared the hell out of us. It was a lot of money and we accepted it out of fear.

If it was a missile that brought down the jet then I could understand that they would not want people to panic. But the way they are handling it is shocking and inexcusable.

My wife and I are outraged and we want people to know how we were treated. This letter is not signed out of concern for ourselves and our family.

In August, 1996, an American Airlines 757 captain on a flight near the Wallops Island NASA Center, Virginia, saw a 'missile' pass his plane. This may have been another attempt to hit a U.S. airline, but it missed. [20]

— Again, the following report is provided by a retired Joint Chiefs of Staff source: "On August 9, 1996 two of more than 70 choppers flying from Fort Campbell, Kentucky crashed at Rock Springs, Wyoming early in the morning. Wyoming citizens' militia sent 11 men out to film it all. The crash site was cordoned off by the Wyoming National Guard, but they gave up after they saw all the cameras. They smashed one person's video camera. They also made the statement that they would no longer 'cover' for federal operations, and left the scene. The 11 men were then captured by the troops that landed in two black C-130s. On the 12th of August, four of the men were released. They were so scared that they were unwilling to say much. They quit the 'militia' program. The other seven have not been heard from. It is alleged that one or more of the seven men were murdered as a 'lesson.' The other six men were released between the 12th and 19th of September. A small newspaper in Wyoming took pictures of the choppers being hauled off by truck. The paper was then 'visited' and warned to keep quiet." A query by the author to one of the men involved remains unanswered. [21]

— In September, 1996, *Encounters* magazine reported a sighting that took place in Tuolomne City, near Twain Harte in California: "Apparently hikers had reported that they had seen a disc-shaped UFO descend slowly to the forest floor and then completely vanish. Curiously though, a few minutes later a helicopter with white lettering on the sides, which spelled 'U.N.,' hovered over the forest meadow. The helicopter flew back and forth as if searching for something before eventually flying off to the west."

This is the type of encounter that causes many UFO buffs to believe that the government is collaborating with extraterrestrial aliens. I find it more likely that the military has craft — perhaps disk-shaped craft — more advanced than they are telling us about. [22]

1997

— An Internet posting of April 10, 1997 inquired: "Often in driving along the diagonal from Boulder [Colorado] to Longmont, I see small helicopters on what look like combat maneuvers. These helicopters are extremely small (Road Warrior heli size), however they look large enough to hold a bomb. Has anyone else seen these helicopters? There are no markings or identifying marks." [23]

— The following is an Internet posting from Brian Ewert, dated April 22, 1997:

> Close friends of ours that live about 15 minutes from our house had an interesting experience. One couple (John and Rita), whose children belong to a religious commune in Canada, were away from their home for a few days last year. Another couple (Bob and Alice), their next door neighbors and also friends of ours, were home, however. One afternoon Bob heard the sound of a very near helicopter. Going out to his deck to see what was going on, he saw hovering closely to John's house, a black helicopter with the side door open, and the soldier inside taking pictures of John's house. When the crew of the black helicopter saw Bob they departed. Bob told John about the event when John and his wife Rita returned home. They thought it was odd and earmarked it in memory. A few days later a man and woman came to John's house posing as sales people of some sort and inquired as to whether or not they would like to sell their home. They had some pictures and explained that the black helicopter was hired from a company that provided an aerial photography service. (Names have been fabricated). [24]

— In June, 1997, a communique was received from Del Bock, the pastor of the Christian Center, in Indianapolis, Indiana. Bock reports that, "...It started one Thursday evening when a gray-headed man in a suit came into our congregation in the middle of service and counted all of our people and walked out. That didn't concern me a great deal until a few months later when I saw three helicopters flying in formation right over our church. It was a Huey, an Apache, and a Huey. The Apache was a fully laden war chopper. They were flying so low I could count the missiles on each side."

Bock says that the fly-overs became almost predictable in their frequency. He mentions two other alarming incidents: "In the early morning I awoke to the sound of a chopper hovering so low it was rattling the windows of our parsonage. It took me about a minute and a half to get clothed and run out my back door to find the chopper hovering over our wooded property. As soon as I saw the chopper, it then slowly flew away."

Concerned about what was going on, he went for a drive in the country with a close friend, and confided a secret word to him, along with instructions about what the man should do if Bock mentioned that word to him: "As soon as I gave him this word," Bock reports, "here comes another low flying Huey and flashed a bright beam on my car in broad daylight three times." Bock later consulted someone "who came with high recommendations in the area of intelligence." Mentioning the most recent chopper incident to him, the man asked him, "Did they flash a beam on you? According to this source, similar incidents have been happening to people all over America, especially to persons with close church affiliations. Bock's source suggested that his property was probably being photographed in case of urban guerrilla warfare. [25]

NOTES:

1.   "Military Incidents Questioned," *The Spotlight,* undated clipping
2.   Anonymous former Joint Chiefs of Staff source, April 23, 1997
3.   "Mysterious black helicopters jangle nerves in N. Arizona," Charles Kelly, *The Arizona Republic,* undated clipping reprinted in the *Patriot Report* information pack for April, 1995
4.   Wilson, Tracy, *Los Angeles Times.* Article reprinted in *Contact,* September 20, 1994
5.   Internet posting at alt.paranet.ufo, Article: 10444, January 10, 1995
6.   Anonymous former Joint Chiefs of Staff source
7.   Smith, Zay N, "Top-Secret Strafing Wakes Whole Suburb," *Chicago Sun Times,* June 13, 1995; Smith, Zay N., "One Suburb Conquered, Army Invades Lemont," June 14, 1995

8. "East Texas county says Army helicopters are spooking cows," Associated Press, May 1995

9. "Letters to the Editor," *Patriot Report,* May 1995.

10. "National News Briefs," *Patriot Report,* September 1995

11. Internet posting, America Online, rec.aviation.military, September 9, 1995

12. Cochran, Peter (pseud.), "They're Back: Black Helicopters Flew to Oregon School to Recruit," *The Spotlight,* November 27, 1995

13. "Unexplained Choppers Hover Over Wyoming," *Media Bypass,* July 1996; Anonymous former Joint Chiefs of Staff source

14. Undated correspondence with anonymous black helicopter witness

15. Anonymous former Joint Chiefs of Staff source

16. Ibid.

17. Ibid.

18. Goddard, Ian Williams, "Military Exercises Terrorize Civilian Population," *The Washington Times,* June 7, 1996

19. Chandler, Chandra, "Strange Sightings in Colorado," *Patriot Report,* June 1996

20. Anonymous former Joint Chiefs of Staff source; Blair, Mike, "Did Sub-Launched Missile Down Civilian Jetliner Off Long Island?", *The Spotlight,* November 18, 1996; Washington Post, September 8, 1996

21. Anonymous former Joint Chiefs of Staff source

22. "Strange UFOs Return to California," *Encounters* magazine, September 1996

23. Internet posting at alt.conspiracy, April 10, 1997

24. Internet posting by Brian Ewert, April 22, 1997

25. *The Excel,* June-July 1997

2

TOXIC SHOCKTROOPS

I n the first Black Helicopter volume, I railed about black choppers spraying toxic substances on populated areas, particularly in areas where political activists live. Since then, other instances of black helicopter spraying have come to light.

A brief recap of earlier incidents is in order:

In June, 1993, the *Patriot Report* stated, "According to reports from American citizens around the nation, military aircraft have been seen spraying over certain residential areas and particular remote targets where patriots live. The reason helicopters and fixed wing aircraft have been spraying those scenes is unknown..."

— On April 30, 1993, a resident of St. Maries, Idaho, saw a military jet flying over a residential area. He noted two curiously shaped canisters located near the wing tips of the aircraft. As the jet flew over at about 1,000 feet in altitude, it sprayed an unknown substance, banked, and then departed. Afterward dead birds were found in the area.

— Also during this period, two dark-colored low flying A-10 Warthog jet aircraft sprayed an unknown substance over populated areas noted as patriot enclaves in Noxon, Montana. Numerous people became sick, and chickens sprayed with the substance died. A few weeks, later a 2-year-old boy became ill and died from an undiagnosable illness. [1]

— Again, in the *Patriot Report*, "Peyton, Colorado land owners fighting with the Federal Housing Authority to keep their land have been sprayed numerous times by black helicopters. They report becoming deathly ill in addition to losing 10 cattle, 7 dogs, and finding 28 dead deer on their property. The local sheriff traced the helicopters back to the National Guard in Denver, Colorado. (The National Guard denies spraying the ranchers' property.)"

— In Couer d'Alene, Idaho a doctor observed aircraft spraying south of the town. Testing the samples, he found them to be biological in nature.

— On May 19, 1994, in the area of Trout Creek, Montana, two jets without insignia performed repeated overflies over a nearby valley. One witness, a woman, became ill with what were described as "radiation" symptoms. Also, within one day, 175 of the woman's pets and chickens died.

The following reports have been obtained since the publication of the first Black Helicopters volume:

— On August 7, 1994, the small town of Oakville, Washington, population 665, experienced the first instance of a toxic assault from above. Tiny gelatinous blobs, "about half the size of rice grains," rained from the sky, blanketing 20 square miles. There were six falls of gelatinous material over the next three weeks. Numerous people became ill within a few days after the fall of strange material, and some animals sickened and died.

Oakville police officer David Lacey was patrolling the town with a civilian friend at 3:00 a.m. on August 7, when the first mysterious fall of gelatinous material occurred. The substance formed a sticky coating on the windshield of Lacey's patrol car, and the officer pulled into a filling station to wipe off the glass. Although Lacey put on a latex glove to wipe off the material, which he describes as being like "Jello," by mid-afternoon he was deathly ill.

"I was to the point where I could hardly breathe," Lacey recalled in an interview. "I started to put together that, possibly, whatever the substance was it made me violently sick and ill, like I never had been before, to the point were I was just totally shutting down." [2]

Oakville resident Maurice Gobeil reported, "I got sick, my wife got sick, my daughter; everybody that lives here got sick."

Beverly Roberts, another resident, said, "Everybody in the

whole town came down with like a flu, and it was a really hard flu, it didn't last seven days, it lasted seven weeks." [3]

Dotty Hearn stepped out of her home after the fall of the unknown substance was over. "I went over and touched it," she recalls, "and it wasn't hail, it was a gelatinous-like material." Hearn also became ill. "I started feeling dizzy, and everything started moving around and around, and it got worse..."

The woman experienced extreme vertigo, vomiting, blurry vision. She collapsed in the bathroom, where she was found later that day by her daughter, Sunny Barclift. Hearn spent four days in the hospital recovering from the strange illness. [4]

Sunny Barclift had moved to Oakville a year before, from Phoenix, Arizona, after working for six years as director of occupational safety and health for the Arizona branch of the National Safety Council. She wrote, in correspondence with the author, "Preceding the first fallout my mother and I witnessed daily fly-overs of black, unmarked military aircraft. We saw both helicopters and what appeared to be cargo planes. Many of Oakville's citizens also report seeing similar aircraft and several witnessed the gelatin fallout."

Barclift included in her correspondence a drawing of a soundless dark, triangular aircraft that was seen flying over Oakville during the same time period. This is the same type of craft that has frequently been observed around the United States, with recent spectacular sightings in Arizona dubbed as UFO encounters. Although the press usually plays up the triangular airplane as a UFO, it is significant that the most frequent sightings have taken place around Air Force bases in California. [5]

A hospital lab technician analyzed the gel that had fallen from the sky and found, surprisingly, that it contained human white blood cells. Another analysis by the State Department of Ecology revealed that unlike human cells, the cells in the gelatinous material had no nuclei.

A sample of the clear gel was forwarded to the Washington State Department of Health, where it was analyzed by microbiologist Mike McDowell. McDowell's report indicated that the substance was teeming with two varieties of bacteria. These were: (1) Pseudomonas fluorescens, found in soil and water, and commonly associated with spoilage of food. Some varieties have been isolated from diseased plants. And, (2) Enterobacter cloacae, found in water, sewage, soil, meat, hospital environments, and on the skin and in the intestinal tract of man and animals.

Early speculation was that the substance was human waste, accidentally jettisoned from an airliner, but FAA regulations stipulate that human waste in aircraft be dyed blue. The substance that dropped from the sky was transparent. There were six falls of the gelatinous material, also negating this explanation. [6]

After the six anomalous skyfalls during a three week period, there were no other confirmed reports of gelatinous falls, although the office of the National Weather Service in the area received word in early August about hot, metallic particles that fell from the sky and burned holes in a child's trampoline. [7]

A related incident during that period was reported by Jim and Kathy Belanger, who were camping at Klaloch, on the Washington coast, in August of 1994. They heard explosions at sea and found globules of clear gel and hundreds of dead crabs on the shore. Kathy Belanger says that when she saw the clear gel on the shore, "I thought at first it was jellyfish, but they didn't look like jellyfish up close." Belanger recalls that she handled the clear gel, and her dog was running on the beach that day. The following day both she and the dog became ill. [8]

Investigation proved that the U.S. Air Force had been dropping live bombs into the Pacific Ocean during this period, about 10 to 20 miles from shore.

Sunny Barclift, who first went public with the Oakville story, explained to the author, "We went to the media with this story because we were told public exposure was the best way to protect ourselves. My mother and I have chosen to withhold some information from the media due to subtle and not too subtle threats from various sources. I will share with you that a high-ranking Army officer stationed at the Pentagon became a family friend preceding the blob experience. He visited us over a period of eight months and claimed he was in the area working on a special project. Specifically he was to 'put into place DOD [Department of Defense] policies relative to FEMA [Federal Emergency Management Agency].' We last saw the 'Colonel' in June 1994 at about the same time Rainier, Washington, (about fifty miles from Oakville) had been scheduled for 'urban combat exercises.' You reported that event in your book [Black Helicopters Over America].

"Our military friend was scheduled to visit us on August 7, 1994, the day of the first fall of blobs. He was a 'no call, no show.' We never heard from him again until last September when he called and questioned my mother [Dotty Hearn] repeatedly about her health and the health of her animals. I met with him in a public place and during our conversation he suggested that I put the experience behind me and go on to other things."

Sunny Barclift writes that the "Colonel" retired from the military in December 1995, but is still employed in the same department at the Pentagon as an independent contractor consultant. He also consults for SRA International, Inc. in Fairfax, Virginia, a company reportedly engaged in creating software for the intelligence community.

Barclift also mentioned that in April, 1997, four men visited her at the restaurant where she works. They asked questions about the fall of gelatinous material, and specifically what information about it would be presented on an upcoming episode of the television show *Unsolved Mysteries*. Barclift said that when they began asking question about things that were not general knowledge about the incident she became suspicious. She copied the license plate on their jeep and had a local police officer run a computerized check on it. The police officer returned with the information that the registered owner of the jeep was from Fort Hood, Texas, and was in "military intelligence."

Barclift sought out information about Fort Hood via the Internet, and found that is the home of the 504th Military Intelligence Brigade, with one unit named the "Blackhawks."

According to her, "Yesterday [May 3, 1997], a military convoy drove through Oakville. All of the military vehicles were camouflage colored with no identifying lettering or numbers, with the exception of one that carried a placard bearing the words 'Blackhawks II.'

Strange falls of gelatinous material that sicken everyone who touches it, taking place in conjunction with military maneuvers, a FEMA program, repeated flights of black aircraft, visits from a mysterious retired military man, and visits from men who are mostly likely military intelligence... The evidence suggests that the government knows far more about the rain of noxious gel on Oakville than they are telling. [9]

— Sometimes the choppers strike extremely close to home. In 1994, in Fallon, Nevada, a silver helicopter approached the farm of "Gil" and his wife "Dawn," two personal friends of the author. They choose not to use their full names in this account.

There had been a good deal of chopper activity in the area for months previous to this, with one or two choppers performing nearby overflies four or five times a week. This time, in the late evening, a Bell helicopter with no apparent insignia made an extremely low pass over the property, at about 50 feet.

Gil went outside the house with binoculars and saw the chopper flying toward his house, shining a searchlight on the ground below. He notes that on the underside of the chopper was a blue bubble of some sort, and speculates that it may have been electronic gear. The chopper flew over the farm for the first time, going west to east.

Although it was dark, Gil noticed that the chopper's searchlight was shining through a mist, the air otherwise being clear. The chopper returned for another overflight, traveling east to west. Gil was now able to confirm that the helicopter was definitely emitting a mist of some sort before it flew away.

The following day, Gil confirmed that in the area that the chopper had overflown there was an approximate 20 foot by 150 foot swathe of dead plants. When the defoliated area grew back in the weeks that followed, the newly-grown plants were gnarled and misshapen.

USE BLACK INK OR
HEAVY PENCIL

Health

Public Health Laboratories
1610 150th Street
Seattle, WA 98155-9701

REFERENCE
BACTERIOLOG

PHYSICIAN NAME	NUMBER	SEX ☐ M ☐ F	AGE
Unidentified substance found at Sunny Barclift residence			

ADDRESS

COUNTY

DATE OF ONSET	CLINICAL DIAGNOSIS	ANTIBACTERIAL AGENTS ☐ NONE ☐ ONE OR MOR

CASE HISTORY, THERAPY OUTCOME

FOR: > DR. Donna Osmond / Director _____ unidentified substance

ADDRESS: > DOH-Labs 1610 N.E. 150th St
STATE ZIP

CITY: > Seattle
WA
AREA CODE & PHONE NO   COUNTY

DESCRIPTION OF SPECIMEN

DATE SPECIMEN COLLECTED

RESULTS TO DATE (Attach results of biochemical & other studies)

SOURCE OF SPECIMEN
☐ HUMAN ☐ ANIMAL (species) _____
☑ OTHER (specify) unknown

TYPE OF SPECIMEN   ☐ CLINICAL ☐ CULTURE
☑ OTHER unknown

ANATOMICAL ORIGIN OF SPECIMEN
unknown

CULTURE ISOLATED   IF MIXED, LIST OTHER ORGANISMS (indicate colony count where applicable)
☐ PURE ☐ MIXED

SERVICES REQUESTED
☐ CONFIRMATION   ☐ INITIAL IDENTIFICATION   ☐ SENSITIVITY

REMARKS
unidentified substance referred to by news media as "blobs"

_____

_____

_____

DO NOT WRITE BELOW THIS LINE

LABORATORY REPORT NO RB	DATE RECEIVED
RB000441	8/31/94

when cultured the unidentified substance grew out the following
microbes ① Pseudomonas fluorescens

② Enterobacter cloacae

DATE OF FINAL REPORT
9-12-94

PERSON WHO COMPLETED TEST   UNIT HEAD
Mike McDowell   Mike McDowell

DOH 305-006 (4/93)

Laboratory test report on substance of Oakville gelatinous fall

OAKVILLE POLICE DEPARTMENT

INCIDENT REPORT

INCIDENT/OFFENSE: Suspious Circumstances

CITATION NUMBER(S): None   **CASE PACKET(S):** none

[REPORTING PARTY]

NAME LAST: Barclift   **NAME FIRST:** Sunny   **MIDDLE INITIAL:**

ADDRESS: ▮

CITY: Oakville   **STATE:** Wa   **ZIP:** ▮   **PHONE:** ▮

← Wrong- Should have been 8-7-94

     DATE OF INCIDENT: 08-14-97   **TIME OF INCIDENT:** 09:40

     DATE OF REPORT: 08-14-97   **TIME OF REPORT:** 10:45

OFFICER(S) ASSIGNED: D.Lacey   **OFFICER NUMBER(S):** 11L4

[SUSPECT INFORMATION- IF APPLICABLE]

SUSPECT LAST: none   **SUSP. FIRST:**   **SUSP. MIDDLE:**

DATE OF BIRTH: **OTHER INFO:**

NARRATIVE OF INCIDENT/OFFENSE: At approx 09:40 hours I was contacted by a
Sunny Barclift of Oakville. She stated that her and her mother had experianced
a translucient jell like substance that had fallen from the sky. Sunny stated
that this had made her mother and herself sick and that her cat had apparently
died from what ever had fallen. She then handed me a glass container with the
jelly like substance she asked if I could have it tested to see what the
substance was. I told her to contact the State of Washington Dept of Ecology
and they would be able to either test or tell her were it should be sent.
I then told sunny that myself and my rider that evening had sampled the same
substance that evening on the windshield of my patrol vehicle. I told sunny to
keep the Police Dept informed on the findings of the substance.

OFFICER SIGNATURE: D.Lacey

Oakville Police Department Incident Report of the gelatinous fall

Within a few days, a dozen dogs and cats on the farm died. The five residents of the farm also became sick, with headaches, weakness, and nausea. The five persons who were at the farm at the time of the over-fly have experienced health problems ever since, and attribute these to the mist sprayed by the helicopter. [10]

— Again, the report of a former member of the Joint Chiefs of Staff, "31 July, 1996... On Wednesday, near Upton, Wyoming (25 miles northeast), ranchers disabled with gunfire and forced down a Blackhawk Model 7 spraying grazing lands and killing the cattle and wildlife... An Air Force chopper came and extracted the foreign crew, most likely not knowing what the U.N. chopper crew was really doing when they were shot down. Vast areas of Wyoming have been 'de-wildlifed' with this spraying campaign, not to mention hundreds of cows killed by the poison which is sprayed on the vegetation, thus killing any animals which eat the stuff." [11]

— Regardless of the above information about the spraying of deadly agents on the populace, livestock, and wildlife, if such incidents are broached to the media they are usually treated as blatant paranoia. The government would not, could not possibly spray the citizens of the United States with deadly viral or other materials. When one examines the facts, however, it becomes apparent that they would, and have.

At Senate hearings that took place in 1977, the Pentagon grudgingly admitted that it had conducted 239 biological warfare tests over populated areas between 1949 and 1969, although other sources place the figure at over 1,000 open air tests of biowarfare agents since the end of World War II. These tests included the release of virulent bacteria into the New York subway system, into the National Airport terminal at Washington, D.C., and onto the Pennsylvania Turnpike.

Although the Pentagon insisted that they used harmless "simulants" of biowarfare weapons in these tests, all of the agents that were used were confirmed by doctors as capable of causing illness and death — and in fact did.

The most commonly used simulant in outdoor tests —

although not the only agent — was Bacillus subtilis, referred to in Army reports as BG. Although the Pentagon has repeatedly told us that BG is harmless, medical literature does not concur with this estimate: BG has been documented to cause infections in the very young, in the elderly, in people with immune deficiencies, or in persons with wounds and prosthetics.

Conveniently for them, over the years the military did not follow up on its experimentation by checking the health of persons in the test areas.

— Edward Nevin was one of 11 patients at Stanford University Hospital who developed Serratia infections in 1950. This illness had never been recorded before at the hospital. But it was 25 years before the family of Nevin learned that at that time the Army had sprayed San Francisco with Serratia marcescens bacteria. Although the family sued for damages, in 1981 a judge ruled in favor of the government.

— In 1953 the Army sprayed the city of Minneapolis, Minnesota with zinc cadmium sulfide, in a simulation of biowarfare attacks. One area that was targeted was the Clinton elementary school, where dozens of former students have experienced unexplainable illnesses in the years that have intervened.

— In 1958 the Army Chemical Corp released a "Summary of Major Events and Problems" that described a series of tests termed "Operation LAC," the largest series ever undertaken by the Army Chemical Corps. Its name was derived from the term "Large Area Coverage." The Army-generated text describes these experiments:

"The test area covered the United States from the Rockies to the Atlantic, from Canada to the Gulf of Mexico. In brief, the Corps dropped a myriad of microscopic particles from a plane, and determined the distance and direction these particles traveled with the wind. The Corps wanted to learn these things: would it be feasible to contaminate a large area by this method, using, for example, BW [biological warfare] organisms, and if so, what logistics would be involved."

The first test took place on December 2, 1957, with a C119 "flying boxcar" dropping particles of zinc cadmium sulfide from South Dakota to International Falls, Minnesota. Testing stations as far away as New York detected the particles.

Although it was known by Army scientists at the time, it is not mentioned in the report that zinc cadmium sulfide is toxic and acknowledged to be potentially carcinogenic.

Another phase of Operation LAC took place in February, 1958. Zinc cadmium sulfide was released from Dugway Proving Ground in Utah. A 200-mile-wide mass of particles released by airplane broadened to 600 miles by the time it reached the Gulf of Mexico.

Two additional tests were conducted in the spring of 1958, with a plane dumping zinc cadmium sulfide from Toledo, Ohio to Abilene, Texas and, in the later test, from Detroit, Michigan, to Springfield, Illinois, then west to Goodland, Kansas.

— Although the Army says that outdoor testing of biological agents discontinued in 1969, one area where the testing has continued is at Dugway Proving Ground, in Utah. Although this top secret facility is located about 70 miles from Salt Lake City, there are communities and Indian reservations located within 20 miles. Ranchers graze their cattle and sheep at the edge of the Dugway property, and highway traffic in the area exceeds 10,000 cars per day.

According to scientists, one horrendous test of nerve gas in 1968 killed 6,000 sheep in Skull Valley, 20 miles from Dugway. Several ranchers in the area also became sick. Although the Army forked out $1 million in damages to ranchers, they have never admitted responsibility. But while the Army will not admit culpability, at least one retired Army Chemical Corps officer who worked at Dugway in 1968 is not so tight-lipped about the death of the sheep. He specifies that the responsible agent was VX, a nerve gas that was released over the base. "We killed them, and we know we killed them," he admits. [12]

NOTES:

1. "Police State Activities in America," *Patriot Report* Info Pack, September 1995
2. Unsolved Mysteries, May 9, 1997

3. Ibid.
4. Ibid.
5. Barclift, Sunny. Correspondence with the author, May 4, 1997; *Unsolved Mysteries;* Paulson, Tom. "They're strange, they're gooey, they're... blobs!" *Seattle Post-Intelligencer,* August 18, 1994
6. Barclift; *Unsolved Mysteries*
7. Paulson
8. Ibid.
9. Barclift
10. Telephone interview with "Gil," June 11, 1997
11. Anonymous former Joint Chiefs of Staff source, April 23, 1997
12. Cole, Leonard. *The Eleventh Plague, The Politics of Biological and Chemical Warfare,* W.H. Freeman and Company, New York, 1996

3

THE MUTILATORS

One of the most controversial aspects of research on the black helicopters is the connection to strange cattle mutilations. In these cases cattle are killed, bovine organs are taken, and operations are sometimes performed with surgical, even laser accuracy. Although cattle mutilations are almost always attributed to extraterrestrial alien intervention when mentioned in the mainstream media, the issue of "BOVMUT," as the FBI dubs it, is not as mysterious as some would have you believe.

Although tabloid television and UFO magazines have had a field day with the issue of the "mutes" and their connection with blood-sucking aliens, the fact that black helicopters are often observed in the area both before and after the mutilations is usually not mentioned. There are, I think, three reasons for this:

(1) "Alien" mutilation makes for more flamboyant "copy" that galvanizes the public with the idea that flying saucers are invading the Earth and ravaging cattle.

(2) The press likes stories that are simple, without complications, working on the theory that the public really doesn't like to think.

(3) Mentioning black helicopters brings in the wild card of government agencies engaged in illegal clandestine operations, and that sometimes opens up a bucket of worms for a broadcaster or publisher.

While I will not rule out that there are truly 'alien' encounters taking place on the earth and elsewhere, my tendency is to pull out Occam's razor and make a few surgical slices of my own, presuming that the connection of UFOs and cattle mutilations with black helicopters is probably of a more terrestrial, although perhaps equally sinister nature in most cases.

Actually, the subject of black helicopters first came to the attention of the public in the late 1960s and 1970s in association with cattle mutilations. Cattle mutilation expert Thomas Adams has written that, "We have something on the order of 200 cases where there have been mystery helicopters sightings in conjunction with mutilations."

Adams does not mention how many records he has of cattle mutilations seen in conjunction with observably "alien" craft. My suspicion is that these encounters are comparatively few. Usually all that is seen are black helicopters or dancing lights in the sky, at least judging from the FBI file on cattle mutilations, obtained through a Freedom of Information Act request. [1]

One oft-voiced supposition is that the black helicopters seen in these instances are piloted by government men investigating cattle mutilations after the fact, and researching their connections to UFOs. Real life X-File guys, see, hot on the trail of the little gray men.

Militating against that view is that the choppers are often observed in the vicinity prior to the mutilation taking place. Additionally, if a government investigation was in progress, wouldn't a ground search of the area of the cattle mutilation be more to the point than a chopper over-fly? In the majority of the accounts that I have read, this does not seem to take place.

Although no hint of it escapes into the popular press or sensationalistic TV accounts with spooky music, there are other clues that suggest that the cattle mutilations, at least some of them, may not be as extraterrestrial as many would have us believe.

In January of 1975, the *Fort Worth Star Telegram* commissioned toxicology tests to be done on a mutilated heifer found near Brownwood, Texas. The test showed a large amount of nicotine in the liver and the blood of the animal. Nicotine is the most common ingredient used in tranquilizer guns. [2]

Many mutilated cattle have been marked with fluorescent paint, presumably to aid identification of specific animals in the dark. Again, this is hardly the modus operandi of gray aliens from Arcturus.

Researcher Ed Sanders, pursuing the cattle mutilation mystery in Colorado in 1975, recalls being "passed by a shiny white van, which was pulling a large shiny white trailer and must have been traveling at 85 miles per hour. I tried to catch up, hoping to copy down the license number, but couldn't keep up. The trailer, I decided, was definitely large enough to carry a small helicopter, and I had just suggested to someone at the sheriff's office that maybe the mute mob was using trucks to transport copters into the vicinity of targeted cattle ranges."

Later, interviewing Trinidad, Colorado District Attorney Louis Girodo, Sanders asked him about staging areas or ground support installations that the black choppers might use.

"Well," Girodo replied, "we know they are ground supported. We know there are maintenance people on the ground with trucks."

Sanders asked Girodo if he knew anything about white vans pulling white trailers.

"Yeah, Texas plates," Girodo replied. "Sure do." Girodo went on to describe an eastern Colorado ranch owned by "some sort of doctor" that was under heavy security that included armed guards, guard dogs, and chained roads. Girodo said, "this was one place where they had taken photos of this particular type of trailer you're talking about." Law enforcement officials requesting to visit the property had been refused entrance.

"We feel that he's using those damn trailers," District Attorney Girodo stated. "That setup is perfect: They've got a van; they've got all the ground support in that van pulling that trailer; and the chopper is in the trailer." [3]

After February 1970 and the accidental release of nerve gas at Dugway Proving Grounds in Utah, experimentation in bacteriological and chemical warfare research was banned in the U.S., with an order issued by Congress to destroy all existing stockpiles of such weapons. Senator Frank Church's Senate Select Committee on Intelligence, in 1976 found that the CIA, for one, had not complied with the order, and had stored enough shellfish toxin and cobra venom to kill hundreds of thousands of people. The CIA also admitted to keeping stockpiled canisters of Clostridium bacteria, of which there are 93 species.

In Utah in 1975, a Department of Agriculture veterinarian found that a mutilated animal that he had autopsied had been injected with some toxin or bacteria. He reports that he was told by his superior at the DOA that if he mentioned the results of the autopsy to anyone he would be fired.

In the fall of 1975, Dr. Susan Colter, director of the Trinidad, Colorado Animal Clinic did a field autopsy on a mutilated heifer whose body had been discovered within 12 hours of its death. Removing the heart, lungs, kidneys and liver from the animal, Dr. Colter sent them to the lab for analysis. Dr. Colter reports that the animals organs had turned to mush. The cause was clostridial infection, the specific agent that the CIA had admitted to stockpiling.

Researcher Ed Sanders reports, "In virtually every state where mutilations have occurred, clostridial infections were found to be the cause of death in some cases. Two well-informed Colorado investigators told me that they felt that the cause of death was being covered up by vaguely-worded laboratory reports prepared by the state government investigators; it has even been charged that reports on the mutes have been suppressed." [4]

District Attorney Girodo reported the instance of a mutilated female buffalo at a zoo in Colorado Springs: "An autopsy was performed," Girodo said, "and traces of chemical foreign to the animal were found in the blood stream. Boy, after that they clamped down on it. They didn't let another word out."

El Paso County Colorado Undersheriff Gary Gibbs, who was in charge of coordinating most of the cattle mutilation investigations in that state, also believes that laboratory results by the Colorado Bureau of Investigation in Denver and at Colorado State University in Fort Collins were hushed up. [5]

Perhaps the only U.S. government official to go public with information suggesting that "mutes" have been injected with bacteria is Dr. Robert Hedelius, a veterinary medical officer for the U.S. Department of Agriculture in Utah. Hedelius investigated the case of a pregnant heifer discovered on September 30, 1975, just outside of Emery, Utah. Professional trackers who examined the scene of the mutilation reported that two persons had been involved, and that they had left the scene of the mutilation and walked along a fence for half a mile until they reached a road, where they had apparently been picked up by companions.

Performing a field autopsy of the heifer, Hedelius found that the death had been caused by "a disease of the Clostridia family. When I did the autopsy, it was apparent that the disease was extremely localized in the neck, an area about the size of a baseball."

Hedelius indicated that initially he had talked to reporters about his findings, but that he had been warned by "higher officials... both state and Federal people. I was told that I was not to talk to any of the news media."

There were alleged attempts to discredit Hedelius' findings. The state veterinarian went on television and said that the mutilation had been done by predators, and that the tests for bacteria were negative. Hedelius' bacterial samples were left in the open air at the laboratory, rendering them useless as proof.

Hedelius is certain about the nature of the mutilation: "I'm sure that whoever did this, shot the animal with a dart gun, and that he used either a culture of the bacteria or a dose of the toxin produced by the bacteria." [6]

During the course of his investigation, Ed Sanders interviewed G.C. Errianne, a private investigator and a former member of an unspecified American intelligence agency. Errianne had been stationed in Europe as a specialist in Russian affairs, and had also worked for the office of the Secretary of Defense in Washington, D.C. Confirming persistent rumors that cattle mutilations were taking place in the course of illegal government biowarfare testing, due to the similarity of the membrane of the eye with "a certain ethnic group," Errianne confirmed that the secret testing was still taking place in the United States.

Errianne remembered that, "in regard to bacteria... There was a meeting at the Bethesda Naval Hospital in 1961; One of the people there was [Secretary of Defense Robert] McNamara. At the time, I worked for the Secretary's office, so it's pretty well substantiated that they did have a meeting in regard to some type of bacteria."

Errianne indicated that these were tests designed to create a specifically anti-Oriental virus.

Reporter Bill Hendrix of KTVX-TV in Salt Lake City provided further confirmation of that diabolic possibility. He indicated personal knowledge of an anti-Oriental biological weapon that had been tested at Dugway. Hendrix also confirmed that on at least two occasions government scientists had traveled to Texas, with other visits possibly to Minnesota, where illegal injections had been performed on cattle.

It is amazing that no protest from the Asian-American community, much less the establishment media, has been raised since this information first appeared, considering that this is a genocidal threat aimed at a specific ethnic group. Where are the concerned citizens protesting this potential latter-day holocaust?

Asian-Americans are apparently not the only ethnic group that has been targeted in military biowarfare testing. Sanders also mentions, "the research may now be aimed against a different human target. One hears talk among mutilation investigators that the mucous membrances of a cow's eye possess properties similar to the mucous membranes of a particular race, and that the cow, therefore, is a perfect subject on which to test the effects of a bacteriological agent." [7]

Is there anyone who might venture a guess as to what this "particular race" might be? And might this provide confirmation for the persistent allegations that the AIDs virus was released as a race-specific depopulation device?

An area of information virtually untouched by researchers is that of human mutilations, and there may be a reason for that. In 1979, in the Bliss and Jerome area of Idaho, two hunters found the nearly-nude body of a man that had been dumped in an extremely remote locale. His lips and sexual organs had been removed and, UFO researcher Don Ecker reports, there were "several other classic mutilation cuts."

Although the man was found in difficult terrain, his bare feet were unmarked, as if he had been transported to the area in a vehicle of some sort. There were no tracks of any kind in the area, however, suggesting the possibility that the corpse may have been dropped from the air.

Researching the murder and mutilation, Ecker employed a friend in the area who was a detective and an active member of the police department. He convinced him to run a search on unsolved human deaths in the Northwestern U.S. using the computerized FBI system. Taking the inquiry back to 1970, the results of the computer search were that there were no unsolved deaths listed for Utah, Nevada, Oregon, and Washington during that period — not even the famed and still quite unsolved Green River killings!

Included in the FBI report was the information that further requests would have to be made by telephone, with authorization. Ecker writes that he had been told by a "prominent ufologist" that there was a lid "screwed down tighter than you would believe in regards to human mutes," and judging from the results of the FBI computer search, that appears to be the case. [8]

NOTES:

1. Adams, Thomas. *The Choppers - and the Choppers*. Project Sigma.
2. Sanders, Ed, "The Mutilation Mystery," *Oui* magazine, September 1976
3. Sanders
4. Ibid.
5. Ibid.
6. Ibid.
7. Ibid.
8. Ecker, Don, "The Human Mutilation Factor," Report obtained from the WUFOC Internet site at http://www.wufoc.com

4

THE ABDUCTORS

Beginning in the late 1960s, black helicopters began to follow and harass UFO witnesses and abductees, in actions reminiscent of their more famous counterparts, the Men in Black.

Black helicopter contacts with UFO witnesses increased in the 1980s, and the craft were often seen in the vicinity prior to UFO abductions — or what the victims believed were UFO abductions. Among well-known abductees reportedly harassed by black helicopters were Betty Andreasson-Luca, Beth Collins, Leah Haley, Kathy Mitchell, Anna Jamerson, Debbie Jordan, Casey Turner, and Whitley Streiber. [1]

Betty Andreasson-Luca's encounters with the black choppers began shortly after her first abduction in 1967. Over the years they were to become an all-too-familiar annoyance to her and her husband, with their repeated low-level fly-overs of their home. Robert Luca describes the craft, saying, "These things are totally black and the windows are tinted so dark that you can't see through them."

Apparently there were other forms of surveillance of the couple taking place as well: "I have no doubt that our phone was tapped," Robert Luca states. "I bought a device that is supposed to detect a tap, and it lit up for our phone but not for one of the others I tested it on."

Betty adds, "Once I picked it up to make an outgoing call and a voice on the other end said 'director's office.' I asked 'director of what?' and the person got all excited and said, 'Oh, I'm sorry,' and hung up." [2]

The black choppers were also often seen in connection with mysterious unmarked vans, with abductees sometimes saying that they had been transported to unknown locations in vans or helicopters, and examined or implanted with possible electronic implants by human doctors.

As opposed to the garden variety UFO abduction sequence of bodily examination taking place within a round "flying saucer" examination room, victims of encounters associated with black helicopters and vans are usually strapped to an examination table or gynecological chair in a cubical room, are given a drink or injected by hypodermic, and are sometimes implanted with a tiny device or have one removed.

Other abductions take place with virtually all of the usual otherworldly trappings, with the single difference that the examinations or implants are conducted at houses, military installations, or laboratories.

Researcher Martin Cannon, in a lecture delivered for a UFO Contact Center International group meeting in 1988, described his investigation of the abduction of a woman whom he called "Veronica." Her abduction was not to a flying disk, but to a specific house in Los Angeles, which upon investigation by Cannon turned out to be inhabited by a scientist who had previously worked on CIA mind control programs.

Comparing Veronica's description of the interior of the house with the recollection of a person who had previously lived there, Cannon found the details to be accurate, confirming that the abduction memory was genuine. [3]

A case I personally investigated in 1993 involved a young woman, a former Satanist who had also been involved with prominent figures in the White Power movement. This young woman claimed that a few years prior, while visiting the leader of a Satanic church in San Francisco, she had been drugged and taken to a hotel. There she had been operated upon by men and women clad in white coats. She had also accompanied the Satanic chief to a location outside of the city, where she was shown a landed UFO at some distance from the highway. This is not an altogether incredible scenario, given the number of persons in military intelligence like Michael Aquino, who have been verified as members, and even heads of, Satanic churches.

Many of the alleged UFO abductees who have also observed black helicopters report on contact with military intelligence personnel, leading one to the somewhat science fictional hypothesis that some faction of government intelligence is conducting mind control experiments that are concealed through hypnotic suggestions and possibly other means of convincing the victims that they have been subject to a UFO abduction. A person who claims that aliens have abducted and implanted him is immediately shunted by the police or other authorities into the nutcase category, providing complete deniability for the agencies that may be conducting this type of experimentation.

Is there any real evidence suggesting that government simulation of UFO abduction and experimentation might actually be taking place? Yes.

The fact that agencies of the government, including the CIA, the Office of Naval Intelligence, NASA, the Atomic Energy Commission, and the Defense Advanced Research Projects Agency, have conducted mind control research for many years has reluctantly been confirmed by these agencies, as well as documented (although the CIA, for one, has admitted to the destruction of thousands of documents detailing its involvement in such research in the 1950s and 1960s).

Although it is a subject virtually untouched by the national media, since at least the 1950s governmental agencies have been involved in clandestine mind control research and experimentation on unwitting persons, in such top secret projects as ARTICHOKE, MK-SEARCH, and MK-ULTRA. These agencies and others, while doing their best to stop word from leaking out about inhumane experimentation into the creation of zombies and mind controlled assassins, have not been entirely able to prevent the release of such revelations.

At least a partial history of government mind control projects is readily available in such books as Marks' *The Search For the Manchurian Candidate,* Bowart's *Operation Mind Control,* and Marchetti's *The CIA and the Cult of Intelligence.* I have written at length on the topic myself in several books.

It is unreasonable to believe that research into this controversial area has been completely discontinued. Reviewing the history of mind control research, it becomes apparent that recent UFO abduction experiences may sometimes be a cover for continuing clandestine — and illegal — research in this area.

Perhaps the most compelling coincidence of UFO abduction and the manipulations of government mind control is in electronic implant technology injected into humans, used for mind control and monitoring. Although it is not widely known, surgically implanted electronic control devices in human beings are a scientific reality that has been perfected for almost fifty years, not some science fictional pipedream.

The most frequent use of the electronic implant technology today is as identification for livestock and pets. At this time more than 3 million animals worldwide have been injected with Destron-Fearing manufactured 'transponders,' an electronic identification tag. In this technology a microchip covered in biomedical grade glass is imprinted with one of over 34 billion available codes. The implant is then injected by needle between the animal's shoulder blades, where it may be scanned later with an electronic wand-like reader.

There have been persistent rumors that soldiers going to the Gulf War were implanted with a monitoring chip. Timothy McVeigh, the man convicted of the Oklahoma City bombing, while in jail complained of the pain caused by a microchip embedded in his buttocks. [4]

Electronic implants for the specific purpose of mind control for humans can be traced in lineage to the 'stimoceiver,' invented in the 1950s by neuroscientist and dystopian visionary Dr. Jose Delgado, funded by the Office of Naval Research, the U.S. Air Force 6571st Aeromedical Research Lab and others. Delgado reflected that, with the advent of the stimoceiver, "Humans can be controlled like robots by push buttons."

Using radio control, Delgado's stimoceiver and later more advanced versions of the same technology have been used to control many aspects of the response of human subjects, including emotions, sensory impressions, hallucinations, and the direct-brain transmission of voices. Of course, information of such research was released in the open literature almost 50 years ago, and it can only be speculated as to advances in current implant technology. I would not be surprised if present-day devices provide total control over the implanted victim. [5]

Those who claim to have had implants against their will are surprisingly numerous. There are x-rays of foreign bodies implanted within the heads of many claimants to prove it, and there are even a number of advocacy groups for people who believe they have received these implants.

Critics of such claims believe that it is unreasonable to think that the government would be engaged in the clandestine electronic implantation of humans, but it also would have been unreasonable to think that the government would inject radioactive compounds into unwitting victims, monitor people infected with syphilis while only pretending to treat them in order to study the ravaging effects of the disease, or purposely infect people with disease viruses. It is now quite clear that the government is a beast without conscience, and capable of anything.

At least one well-known UFO abductee speculates that his experiences may have something to do with this kind of manipulation. Whitley Streiber, self-described abductee and the author of *Communion* and other bestselling books detailing his travails with the aliens, at the 1996 Gulf Breeze UFO Conference broached the possibility that he might be the subject of mind control operations by U.S. intelligence agencies.

Streiber believes that he has two implants in his body, one in an earlobe, another in a little finger. He cites unusual intelligence tests administered to him as a child as a possible tip-off to life-long monitoring, tests that he says he does not know who administered to him. He speculates that his experiences with supposed aliens may have actually been broadcast to him through these implants. [6]

Other aspects of Streiber's background are evocative. His fiction novel *Black Magic,* released prior to his more famous *Communion* series, is about extremely low frequency radiation (ELF) used for mind control and the enhancement of ESP capabilities. Streiber dedicates the book to the military intelligence operatives from whom he obtained the information in the book. Early in his career Streiber worked on a film about The Process Church, the Scientology-offshoot organization that Charles Manson allegedly was a member of, and which is said to engage in mind control indoctrination. [7]

Significantly, in many UFO abduction cases, the victims claim that implantation is done transnasally. This is also the most common means documented for installing intelligence agency, rather than alien, implants. Coincidence? Reports of alien implantation also precisely parallel in time experimentation into brain implants by researchers in the pay of American intelligence agencies. I do not know of even a single individual claiming alien mind control implants prior to Delgado's invention of the stimoceiver.

It is also extremely strange that if the mind control implants are performed by extraterrestrials that they are of such a primitive nature. This alien race, that we are led to believe may be thousands if not millions of years more advanced than human culture, would seem to be able to abduct people without any memory of the event whatsoever, and to create an implant that was totally undetectable once in place. Why are the aliens still stumbling along with technology no more advanced than that tinkered together by the CIA in the '50s?

Another form of mind control that the government has experimented with is the broadcasting of extremely low frequency electromagnetic radiation (ELF) at targeted human subjects. Helmut Lammer, a researcher into the black helicopter/UFO abduction connection, cites a recent military publication called the *New World Vistas,* undertaken by the USAF Scientific Advisory Board, and published in June, 1996:

> In this publication, military scientists suggest that the development of electromagnetic energy sources, the output of which can be pulsed, shaped, and focused and coupled with the human body will be able to: 1) allow one to prevent voluntary muscular movements, 2) control emotions and actions, 3) produce sleep, 4) transmit suggestions, 5) interfere with both short-term and long-term mem-

ory, and 6) both produce and delete an experience set [i.e. to simulate a reality].

Although these sorts of experiments are proclaimed to be highly experimental and of limited success in their application, that is the standard cover story of the military when attempting to keep their work secret. In fact, this kind of body and mind alteration by ELF waves, usually performed on unknowing subjects, has also been going on since at least the 1950s.[8]

Persons who have experienced black helicopter fly-overs and harassment sometimes also believe that they have been electromagnetically irradiated in some way. This is the case with Rex Niles, a defense subcontractor. Niles cooperated with authorities investigating defense industry kickbacks and believes he was targeted with electronic mind control harassment as a result.

According to the *Los Angeles Times,* "He [Niles] has produced testimony from his sister, a Simi Valley woman who swears that helicopters have repeatedly circled her home. An engineer measured 250 watts of microwaves in the atmosphere outside Niles' house and found a radioactive disc underneath the dash of his car.

"A former high school friend, Lyn Silverman, claimed that her home computer went haywire when Niles stepped close to it." [9]

Another account suggesting electromagnetic radiation and implanting was received by the author in 1995, and is reprinted with permission:

> Two summers ago I was at Carnegie, which is in the hills between Tracy and Livermore in California. I went to an area I had been before, where I had done some target shooting. I had fired about 20 rounds when I decided to have lunch, which I had brought with me. I fixed lunch on a rock formation near the foundation of the old brick factory and while eating, I caught something out of the corner of my eye. I hadn't heard anything, but suddenly there was an object floating across the fields of the valley. I left my lunch and walked down to the field. When I got closer I realized it was a

helicopter. My first thought was that I was in trouble for target practicing with my pistol, but I had seen others practicing in the area before, so I wasn't sure what to think.

It was flat black and rather insect-like in appearance, with a wide, bulbous head and a long thin tail. It had no rear propeller that I could see, and the rotor on top made no discernible noise. Also, there was no apparent landing gear.

As I walked toward the helicopter it turned its nose to me. I expected it to land. The helicopter came directly over me, and suddenly a bright light shone from the middle of the craft, like a halogen worklamp. I felt like I was being cooked. I fell to the ground, and it was as if my body was asleep but my brain was awake. I don't know how long I laid there still, and completely terrified, but two men dressed in black with black watchcaps appeared. My first thought was that they were there to help me. One shined what looked like a penlight in my eyes, a stainless steel elongated tube with a 'tranquil' light, I don't know of a better way to put it. I felt something cold in my left ear. The other man was apparently checking my pulse, and they were talking, but I couldn't understand them. My hearing was coming in and out with buzzing and ringing.

That is all I remember. I woke up and it was dark, and I was alone again. I ran back to my car, which was parked at least half a mile away. I drove to a truck stop and I called my wife. I don't know if she believed me, but she talked me down a bit so I could make it home.

A lot of people have asked me what I think those guys did to me and if some UFO-type thing was implanted. I think they were testing out some new technology, and seeing what effect it had on me. I can say it was very frightening, and the idea that there may be something in my head that shouldn't be there still scares the hell out of me. To tell you the truth, I really don't want to know what they did to me. I believe that it is the duty of our government to develop effective weapons to defend our way of life, but I don't think anyone wants to be their guinea pig. [10]

The evidence that we are seeing suggests a startling possibility that has been slow in dawning upon UFO researchers: that the military is counterfeiting alien abduction experiences to cover up mind control operations on unwitting individuals.

NOTES:

1. Cooper, Vicki, "Black Helicopters Dog UFO Witnesses," *UFO* magazine, Volume 4, Number 1, 1989
2. Holaham, David, "Betty and Bob Luca - their claims of contact - with extraterrestrial beings," *Connecticut Magazine,* August 1988
3. Cannon, Martin, "UFOs and Mind Control," transcript of a talk given for the UFO Contact Center International, 1988, copy in the author's possession
4. Crosby, Lisa, "The Microchip Injection," *Paranoid Women Collect Their Thoughts,* Paranoia Publishing, Providence, Rhode Island. Ed. Joan D'Arc.
5. Delgado, Jose. *Physical Control of the Mind.* Harper & Row, New York, 1969; Cannon, Martin, "The Controllers: A New Hypothesis of Alien Abductions," *MUFON UFO Journal,* Number 270, October 1990
6. "False Miracles in the Sky: Is the U.S. Military in the Business of Hoaxing UFOs?," *The Devil's Advocate,* Issue number 5
7. World Watchers International, undated clipping
8. Lammer Ph.D, Helmut, "Preliminary Findings of Project MILAB: Evidence for Military Kidnappings of Alleged UFO Abductees," obtained on the Internet, 1996
9. Cannon, Martin, "The Controllers"
10. Fair, Allen, correspondence with the author, October 3, 1995

A housewife took this photo of a Russian Hind-D attack helicopter flying over her home north of Gulfport, Mississippi, where they are located at a National Guard base.

Revised Army Reserve Jurisdictions corresponding to FEMA designations.

Black helicopter observed in Texas. (Photo: Blackhawk)

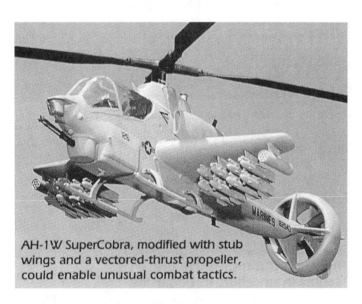

AH-1W SuperCobra, modified with stub wings and a vectored-thrust propeller, could enable unusual combat tactics.

Black helicopters over Michigan, 1994. (Photo: *The Spotlight*)

Chinese military action in the Taiwan Strait, March 25, 1996.

Russian-made U.N. vehicles in Saucier, Mississippi
(Photo: *The Spotlight*).

Russian fire control radar unit photographed in Michigan. One vehicle in a trainload. (Photo: *The Spotlight*)

Russian frog missile and launcher seen en route in Tennessee (Photo: *The Spotlight*).

Russian Ilyushin IL-76 candid refueling tanker, photographed at Barksdale Air Force Base in Shreveport, Louisiana. Note the red star on the tail (Photo: *The Spotlight*).

Russian military equipment headed to Elgin Air Force Base in Florida in 1994 (Photo: *The Spotlight*).

Russian manufactured trucks painted *U.N. White,* photographed in Saucier, Mississippi (Photo: *The Spotlight*).

WARNING

THIS IS A U.S. CUSTOMS
BONDED WAREHOUSE

Whoever maliciously enters a
U.S. Customs Bonded Warehouse
with the intent to remove there-
from any merchandise or unlawfully
removes any merchandise from
U.S. Customs Service custode
or control shall be guilty of a
Federal crime and shall be fined
not more than $5,000 or impri-
soned not more than 2 years,
or both.

Russian-made truck photograghed in Saucier, Mississippi (Photo: *The Spotlight*).

Black helicopter (Photo: Robert A. Luca).

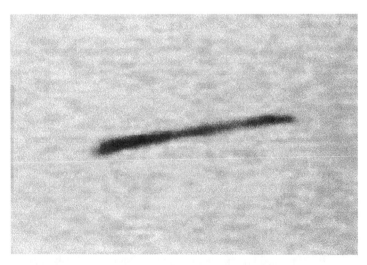

Unidentified object in black helicopter photograph (Photo: Robert A. Luca).

5

WHOSE CHOPPERS ARE THEY?

Evidence suggests the primary source for the black helicopters is the strikeforce of the gradually expanding national police network in the United States. The black helicopters are the "storm troopers" for the tightening of surveillance and armed intervention in 21st century America. And intervene they have, with MJTF forces and black helicopters involved in such recent horrendous shows of overkill as Waco and Ruby Ridge.

This group is headed up by FEMA, the Federal Emergency Management Agency, and Forces Command, headquartered in the same building as FEMA in Atlanta, Georgia, with another task force run out of California. FEMA is really nothing more than a bit of bureaucratic slight-of-hand allowing the military, military reserves, the U.N. and others to police the U.S. in what seem to be a myriad of "black operations," i.e. projects that do not show up on documentation of funding requests to Congress.

These actions, using the military to police the U.S., violate the posse commitatus provision of the Constitution, stipulating the military will not intervene domestically. Not to be surprised, however; since the beginning of this century, America has been involved in a gradually escalating devolution from a relatively democratic republic, to a fiefdom of the flat-out globalist state.

Originally, the Constitution was successful in fractionalizing power throughout government, preventing any single segment from assuming dictatorial power. That is no longer the case. As Gary Allen explains in the classic, *None Dare Call It Conspiracy,* "In order to have a dictatorship one must have a single branch holding most of the reins of power. Once you have this, dictatorship is inevitable." [1]

Now, as unlawful police actions and constitutional encroachments proceed at the speed of a runaway train, we see power in
America devolving to the rule of force and executive fiat rather
than Congressional, or popular authority. Now power is
hoarded and pilfered through unlawful executive order. The
Constitution itself, virtually the only guarantee of the rights of
the American people, has been thrown out in repeated, now
routine tramplings of individual rights.

Now government does whatever it can get away with,
which, given a compliant press and a Congress which looks the
other way, is virtually anything. With continued calls for a new
constitutional conference, the Constitution may soon be thrown
out altogether if something is not done.

There is a self-reinforcing loop here. With the evolution
toward top-down dictatorial control has developed protest from
the populace, thus further need for a heightened internal security
force — the black helicopters and black-uniformed MJTF stormtroopers. These are utilized in much the same way as Russia's
Internal Security is wielded by their interior ministry: to keep a
thumb ground down on the people.

With the worsening of economic conditions in America due
to excessive taxation and control, and elitist violations of American sovereignty like the NAFTA and GATT treaties, the American worker's earning power is gradually being brought into
parity with the Third World technologists of adobe. Heavier
firepower — black helicopters, for one — is now needed to
suppress unrest among the people, or at least so those at the
highest levels of government think.

I recently spoke to one source who had gotten a "hands-on"
education in the black helicopters: he had climbed onto a black
chopper, one of two stored in a hangar at a military airbase near
where I live. Contrary to reports of insignia visible only from a
close distance, and deep olive drab coloration, these choppers
were jet black, and had no insignia whatsoever. Stored inside
the cockpit, my informant said, there were flak jackets and hand
grenades. [2]

One location from which black choppers sorties are

launched with great frequency is Fort Campbell, Kentucky, and the U.S. Army's 101st Airborne Division. The 160th Special Operations Aviation Regiment, known as the 160th SOAR, are termed the "Nightstalkers," and employ the motto, "Death Waits in the Dark."

Another reason for the secrecy of the black helicopters is that numerous sorties have been flown by members of the Organized Crime Drug Enforcement Task Force, an alliance of the military and local police forces, involved for several years in anti-drug raids and reconnaissance around the country.

Again, given the posse comitatus provision of the Constitution, it is understandable why these flights have been covert — they are unlawful. Since the enactment of the equally unconstitutional 1995 Crime Bill, however, any federal agency is allowed to liase in "crime task forces" with local agencies, and so the need for keeping these activities under wraps has greatly diminished. Now the military actively and openly joins forces with state and county law enforcement in heavy-handed "drug suppression" assaults by black chopper and black stormtroopers sans insignia.

As noted in *High Times* magazine, "The Defense Department will spend more than $720 million on domestic counter-narcotics operations this year, and millions more on other assistance to civilian law enforcement. The Pentagon says federal law allows the military to aid civilian police as long as troops do not perform arrests, searches, seizures or other direct constabulary duties. But it appears that in the post-Cold War order — as the vast U.S. military machine begins to pull back its overseas tentacles — the war is coming home...

"The Army National Guard's marijuana control program has been providing military helicopters — usually black and sometimes unmarked — to local law enforcement coast to coast since the big 1988 federal anti-drug legislation." [3]

The drug enforcement connection of some of the black choppers has been further verified by the Department of Transportation, writing to Senator Hank Brown of Colorado in response to his questions about black chopper flights around

Lakewood, Colorado. The Department of Transportation told him that the choppers were Drug Enforcement Agency and U.S. Army Special Operations helicopters. [4]

Black helicopters of military origin and multi-jurisdictional command use a paint called "CARC," that is radar absorbent and easily cleansed of biowarfare agents. Although the cover story, repeated by the military and government mouthpieces in the media is that all black helicopters are actually painted the deep olive drab with light ID letters and numbers seen in profusion at military bases and at air shows, there are also flat black models with no insignia whatsoever, obviously flying in violation of FAA regulations and engaged in secret forays within the U.S. [5]

A recurring report is that some of the black helicopters are silent. This is borne out by information on advanced types of choppers — of which there are a variety currently aloft. One type of 'quiet mode' black chopper employed nationwide (and by SOAR) is termed the NOTAR, resembling the Hughes 500 helicopter, only with a larger tail boom. Instead of a tail rotor, the NOTAR has a shrouded fan in the tail cone, with air blowing the length of the cone. Air is directed out of the side of the cone by a movable slot in the tail cone, counteracting the torque of the main rotor, and making the craft extremely maneuverable as well as much quieter than conventional helicopter models.

Another, even more high tech silent chopper was reported in the *Las Vegas Review-Journal,* in February of 1995. According to statements of a former worker at Groom Lake Air Force Base, a black budget stealth helicopter was being tested at this facility as early as 1990. The code name for the helicopter was "T.E.-K," which stood for "Test and Evaluation Project K."

The former worker at Groom Lake reported that the chopper was olive drab, riveted, and angular, with gull wing doors. An account in the Vegas paper quotes experts as saying, "Light, quiet and stealthy helicopters could be used for clandestine 'Rambo-type missions,' quick-in, quick-out assignments without being noticed." [6]

A report of another extremely high tech chopper is provided

by *Popular Mechanics* magazine. The craft is termed the "Compound SuperCobra," and it is reported that, "Although the Army grounded the concept 30 years ago while developing its original attack choppers, the compound helicopter may rise again. Piasecki Aircraft Corp. has blueprinted modifications to the AH-64A Apache and AH-1W SuperCobra, and is testing them in simulation exercises at Boeing Helicopter facilities.

"The stub wings provide higher speeds and agility by unloading the main rotor. Meanwhile, the vectored-thrust ducted propeller lends thrust and an anti-torque function. It also permits some unique maneuvers, such as raising the helicopter's nose by 27 degrees, while maintaining a hover. Piasecki aims to fly a modified SuperCobra under a research contract with the Marines." [7]

One startling capability that may be possessed by some of the black helicopters — but which is usually reported in the media to have been caused by UFOs — is the disabling of automobile electronics from a distance.

On July 18, a man was driving his car on Interstate 15, near Farmington, outside of Salt Lake City. Driving southbound he observed four black helicopters, and as he drove in the direction of the choppers the engine in his vehicle stopped. There was no sputtering of the motor, as if it had run out of fuel, just a sudden ceasing of combustion.

The man steered the vehicle off the highway, then attempted to re-start it. At this time he noticed that most of the other cars on the highway had also stopped, but oddly enough, an older model car was still negotiating its way through the stalled vehicles. Traffic in the vicinity was held up for about an hour, then suddenly all the stalled vehicles were able to be started again. Again, at this time the man noticed four black helicopters flying nearby.

Although the media did not touch this incident, several witnesses have come forward describing the event. The existence of this previously secret technology is verified by a report from the Associated Press wire service:

"A stolen van speeds down a busy interstate highway, but

police don't even think about a high speed pursuit. Instead, they push a button.

"Using technology that will be tested next month, officers would be able to stop a car by sending an electrical charge that disables a vehicle's electronics and shuts off its engine. The 'car-stopper' was announced by federal officials yesterday as a way to employ technology first developed during the Cold War against criminals who try to evade capture by speeding away from authorities." [8]

For covert flights of black helicopters within the United States, an alternate communications system must be employed. Electronically linking the black helicopters launched by the military are a number of high tech communications networks. One source details a system that may be used by the black helicopters:

"GeoNet, a high speed bit-oriented VHF datalink with air-to-air communications which can accommodate satellite and transponder Mode S, has a range of 1,000 miles. The GeoNet is based on adaptive broadcast-dependent surveillance datalink, a wireless high-speed communication protocol that supports the transportation of text and graphics data. When an equipped helicopter or vehicle enters a geoLink, it instantly transmits its vehicle tag, applications data and any messages to other vehicles located outside the geoLink area. Such messages are passed between any aircraft or vehicle within listening range using a special protocol." [9]

Some of the black helicopters may now or in the near future have no pilots at all. According to the *Wall Street Journal,* "In the skies above cities will soon appear some tiny, pilotless aircraft that might be mistaken for model airplanes. They're not. Inside will be high-resolution cameras that can make out small objects from hundreds of yards, infrared detectors that can see in the dark — and maybe even chemical sensors that can pinpoint drugs in the area.

"They're called Unmanned Aerial Vehicles (UAVs), and they're going to be used to fight crime and they're real, not science fiction. And they're just one small ripple in the wave of the future. Across the country police agencies are extending the long arm of the law by using eerily invasive high technology to speed the work of catching crooks, tracking stolen goods, and snooping on suspected wrongdoers." [10]

As many researchers have guessed, if some black choppers are in the business of stopping drug trafficking, apparently some are involved in the trade itself. Researcher Eugene Austin, in correspondence with the author, has stated that,

> In 1980, I was shot at by occupants of an unpainted, unmarked helicopter operating out of Grand Junction, Colorado Airport. It was owned by [title deleted], a CIA 'cover' from Dover, Delaware. I shot back at the rotor with a high powered rifle and contacted local law enforcement and FAA.
>
> Locals told me that the choppers were used by BLM personnel who flew cocaine from South America to Grand Junction in a DC-4, then used the choppers to fly the stuff to 24 Mile Canyon where it was picked up by 'mules.'
>
> The operation was the source of the Richard Chase serial killing, which included the murder of a BLM supervisor who was trying to shut it down. There was a strong Miami link. Chase was murdered in his death row cell.
>
> There were dozens of 'UFO sightings' and ten or so horse mutilations, all used to keep the unwashed public away from 24 Mile Canyon and Bookcliff Mesa. Partly because I am not part of the 'ooga-booga crowd,' (People who believe UFOs are spaceships piloted by funny-looking ETS) FAA talked freely. They say that there are several thousand unmarked choppers that inspectors are forbidden to investigate or prosecute. It is common knowledge that they are used in cocaine trafficking by CIA, FBI and other federal agencies.
>
> Animal mutilations/UFOs are disinformation designed to divert attention, discredit researchers and terrorize law enforcement officers.

Who is manning the black helicopters? One unconfirmed report alleges that the pilot of the craft are foreign:

> The good news is that the United Nations cannot find enough

qualified, and unpatriotic pilots amongst the U.S. citizenry to reach their goals. The bad news is that they have set up an organization on American soil to smuggle out-of-work Communist pilots into the country. Hiding under the techno-sounding name 'Global Exchange,' they import pilots to their headquarters in San Francisco, California (okay, so it's not 'real American' soil, like Idaho). The pilots are then furnished with fake IDs (operatives within the Democratic Party provide the blank IDs from the various states they control), English language courses, and a selection of credit cards. When the pilots are sufficiently acclimatized, they are shipped out to their 'cover' assignments, to be contracted when there is a training sortie taking place (or when the Takeover happens)." [11]

At least some black helicopter pilots are willing to talk about what they are doing. One apparently authentic chopper pilot, Mike, posted the following response to a question about black helicopter activity on the Internet:

I happen to fly the little black helicopters you are talking about and have for some time. I would like to point out some facts. I have not been assigned to fly over houses and shoot weapons nor have I been told to harass people. The government is not the best in the world but we in the military have better training to do than harass Pittsburgh. First Army helicopters are painted olive drab which to me is the same color as black, like navy blue. The buzz numbers the FAA requires are on the aircraft just painted black for low visibility. We train to perform combat operations, flying in a brightly painted aircraft is not tactically sound. Only at Fort Rucker are helicopters painted with high visibility paint and buzz numbers. As far as anyone is concerned it's your money. Take a picture if you want. I normally smile if I see you.

Lastly, if any pilot flies recklessly or what seems that way, report him to the FAA nearest military base, or other airport. Chances are he was on ATC and they have his tail number. As far as Pittsburgh is concerned [where 'mock warfare' maneuvers were conducted], there is a National Guard base in the area and they may be alarming people. — Mike [12]

As Mike assures us, "I have not been assigned to fly over

houses and shoot weapons nor have I been told to harass people."

Should that allay the concerns of people who have been shot at, harassed, or sickened with the spray of unknown chemicals by black choppers?

NOTES:

1. Allen, Gary (with Larry Abraham). *None Dare Call It Conspiracy.* Concord Press, Seal Beach, California, 1991
2. Anonymous, March 14, 1997
3. Weinberg, Bill, "Black Helicopters are Real!", *High Times,* June 1996
4. *McAlvaney Intelligence Advisor,* reprinted in the *Patriot Report,* November 1993
5. "Subject: Chemical Agent Resistant Coating (CARC)," *USACHPPM Information Paper,* August 1992
6. Greene, Susan, "Ex-Worker Describes Stealth Copter," *Las Vegas Review-Journal,* February 26, 1995
7. "Compound SuperCobra," *Popular Mechanics,* January 1996
8. "Subject: Test of Electronic Shutdown of Autos," Salt Lake Fax Network, original in author's possession; Undated Associated Press clipping, reprinted in the *Patriot Report,* November 1996
9. C.I.A. Newsletter, October 1996
10. "Techno-Cops," *Wall Street Journal,* December 12, 1990
11. "Little Black Helicopter Page," Internet
12. Obtained from the Internet, March 10, 1997

6

POLICE STATE AMERICA

Providing essential perspective on what is going on in this country is background on FEMA, the Federal Emergency Management Agency. In 1974, a time of great social unrest, Ronald Reagan (then governor of California) commissioned a study analyzing ways to change city and county governments. This study was termed the Houlihan Report, and it drew a number of interesting conclusions. Quoting,

"There must be a climate for change in order for the restructuring of local government to occur, whether this restructuring involves drastic reform, reorganization, modernization, or a minor administrative realignment. While the following does not represent an exclusive list, the factors mentioned here are those which most often create such a climate:

A. A collapse of government's ability to provide needed services;
B. A crisis of major magnitude;
C. A catastrophe that has a physical effect on the community;
D. The corruption of local officials;
E. The high cost of government and the desire for a higher level of services.

The report surmised, "Some change will occur, in one form or another, if any of the first four factors (collapse, crisis, catastrophe, or corruption) are present, especially when they are of major dimension." [1]

Utilizing this "climate for change," FEMA was birthed without the approval of Congress through Executive Order 12148, and was designed to liase with the Department of Defense. Although FEMA is ostensibly empowered to throw a life preserver to the populace in times of natural catastrophe, a

Congressional study showed that the agency has been spending 12 times as much on "black operations"—the specifics of which are unavailable for public scrutiny—as for projects relating to national emergencies. Obviously, FEMA's mandate is considerably wider than what is expressed publicly.

As an instance, $1.3 billion in FEMA funds have secretly been used—unbeknownst except to 20 members of Congress— in the construction of underground bases in the COG (Continuity of Government) program, insuring that brass and the bureaucrats survive in the event of an emergency.

FEMA's latitude for control is vast, and depends upon a number of executive orders which, although mentioned in the first volume of this series, deserve to be mentioned again. These executive orders include:

> EO 10995, authorizing the suspension of the freedom of speech and the commandeering of all U.S. communications media.
>
> EO 10997, authorizing the takeover of electrical systems and other fuel sources.
>
> EO 10998, providing for the government control of food sources, including farms.
>
> EO 10999, authorizing the control or confiscation of the nation's transportation sources, public and private.
>
> EO 11000, which gives the government the right to form work brigades of citizens.
>
> EO 11001, providing for the takeover of all health, education, and welfare functions and facilities.
>
> EO 11002, authorizing a national registry of the population.
>
> EO 11003, authorizing the takeover of all aircraft and airports.
>
> EO 11004, which gives government the mandate to relocate populations from one area to another.
>
> EO 11005, which provides for the government to take over railways, waterways, and public storage facilities.
>
> EO 12148, authorizing FEMA to take over the executive functions of the government.

FEMA's powers were also augmented by President Carter in 1979, so as to incorporate:

— The National Security Act of 1947, allowing the relocation of industries, government, and economic activities.

— The 1950 Defense Production Act, providing the President virtually unlimited control over every aspect of the economy.

— The Act of August 29, 1916, authorizing the Secretary of the Army, during wartime, to commandeer any transportation systems.

— The International Emergency Economic Powers Act, authorizing seizure of property.

Given the above executive orders—during times of emergency or times of pretended emergency—FEMA can assume the reins of the government, taking complete charge of the country. With precautions, that might almost be a reasonable function in times of national emergency, but as it exists FEMA is a back door bypassing the Constitution, and that should be enough to give any American cause for concern.

At the birth of FEMA, Louis Giuffrida, the head of the Army's Combat Development Command, was tapped to head up the organization. Giuffrida had run the California Specialized Training Institute (CSTI), in San Luis Obispo, training more than 27,000 officials in the Civil Disorder Management Course. The course drilled nervous bureaucrats on such topics as:

— Unrest in Modern Society
— Control Force Intelligence
— Dissent, Disruptions, and Violence
— Contemporary Insurgency
— and, Mass Arrest Procedures [2]

In April, 1984, in a move that was completely unknown to the public, President Reagan signed Presidential Directive Number 54, instructing FEMA to take part in a secret national "readiness exercise." Dubbed REX 84, the plan was drawn up by Lieutenant Colonel Oliver North. Conducted in total secrecy behind metal security doors at the FEMA building in Washington, D.C., a tight clique of persons wearing a red crucifix lapel pin were the only persons allowed into the REX 84 brainstorming operations. FEMA's REX 84 was the basic blueprint of what we all fear, and what the ostriches and agents of the controlled media insist could never happen.

Rex 84 called for the suspension of the Constitution, and the declaration of martial law, with FEMA taking over the control of government, while the assumption of control of state and local government would be done by the military, under the direction of FEMA. Congress was not empowered to review the institution of martial law by FEMA until six months after the fact, and under FEMA provisions there exists no protocol for the restoration of constitutional rule.

Rex 84 authorized the deputizing of U.S. military and National Guard for law enforcement within the United States. A blueprint was drawn up to take into custody 400,000 illegal Central American immigrants, who would then be interned in ten detention centers located in military bases within the country. These detention centers were constructed, and have been maintained in readiness to this day. Also planned, in the event of rioting, was the relocation to "assembly centers or relocation camps" of 21 million Black Americans.

FEMA has been accused of engaging in other secret military operations, as when in June 1983, investigators for the Senate were told of C-130 and C-141 cargo planes then en route to Texas. The planes had been refitted with troop seats, and Senate investigators at the time voiced suspicions that something very strange was going on without notification of Congress. The predominant belief was that American soldiers were secretly being flown to Central America to fight a secret war.

One Senate aide said, "The flight times were just right for a trip down there and back. Yet when we asked for information, FEMA said it was COG [Continuity of Government program], and refused to discuss it. Not even the intelligence committees could find out what was going on." [3]

Later, FEMA was ready to step in and save the day during Operation Desert Storm in Iraq. Plans were set in motion for the organization to set up bases in the U.S. without the necessity for obtaining prior permission of local and state authorities. FEMA again stood ready to intervene during the Los Angeles riots, which took place after announcement of the Rodney King brutality verdict. No word of the FEMA contingency plan for relocation camps for Blacks was released via the media.

Over the years FEMA has continued to expand its jurisdiction. Since September 1996, The U.S. Army Reserve Command (USARC) has been functionally restructured to conform to the designated regional structures of FEMA, making it easier for FEMA to assume control of this organization in times of "emergency." An official press release reports that this restructuring took place "in a move that will enhance its ability to support domestic missions and improve its readiness to go to war."

The report goes on to say, "An important feature of the plan is that it will permit the Army Reserve to provide greatly enhanced federal military support to civilian authorities and other federal agencies for domestic assistance missions. The Regional Support Command boundaries coincide with the Standard Federal Region (SFR) boundaries used by all federal agencies, including the Federal Emergency Management Agency."

A source in the Army Reserve informs us that this restructuring "eliminates the present U.S.-based regional headquarters called Army Reserve Commands (ARCOMS) and replaces them with 10 Regional Support Commands (RSCs), which will report directly to the U.S. Army Reserve Command Headquarters in Atlanta, Georgia, and three Regional Support Groups (RSGs) which will report to the RSCs." [4]

An official Army Reserve document reports that martialling the Army Reserves under the FEMA is "aimed to transform the Army Reserve, not into a smaller version of the Cold War force, but into a new Army Reserve, able to provide fully ready units for America's Army of the next century, and to provide a greatly enhanced capability in support of domestic actions."

The 10 FEMA regional jurisdictions, governed by directors appointed by the President, are outlined in a secret Army manual (FM 41-10), Civil Affairs Operations, that carries a "Destruction Notice" on its front cover: "Destroy by any method that will prevent disclosure of contents or reconstruction of the document." There are several reasons the manual is sensitive, but one is that it includes a generic concentration camp blueprint. [5]

The 10 Regional Support Commands are: RSC 1, Massachusetts; RSC 2, New York; RSC 3, Pennsylvania; RSC 4, Alabama; RSC 5, Minnesota; RSC 6, Arkansas; RSC 7, Kansas; RSC 8, Utah; RSC 9, California; and RSC 10, Washington. Regional Support Groups are located at Fort Jackson, South Carolina; Fort Benjamin Harrison, Indiana; and San Antonio, Texas. [6]

Equally with FEMA, the increasing centralization of police power in America poses a threat to freedom. The recent "Omnibus Crime Bill" passed by Congress is nothing more than a transparent ruse by which the federal bureaucrats can consolidate control over local and state police agencies.

As specified in the crime bill, 100,000 new police officers will be hired using newly-requisitioned funds, but this is not going to be "Andy of Mayberry" and the restoration of the peaceful days of yore. These forces will be controlled by federal authorities, not by local police departments.

Given that these federal police officers have no ties with the local communities in which they will be enforcing laws, this is tantamount to the creation of a national mercenary force that will be wielded at will by the executive branch or FEMA, in the case of an emergency.

FEMA is apparently the source of the black helicopters that have been flying in and out of a secret mountain base in Napa County, California, since the mid 1990s. Aerial photographs taken by investigators in 1995 have shown that a new, freshly graded road has been constructed in the area, along with a heavily fortified underground facility, and several cement bunkers located above the ground. There is also a communications tower at the location, with eight or ten microwave dishes pointed into the sky.

Over 200 pages of classified and unclassified documents

relating to the Napa base obtained by investigators show that the underground site was built to replace the functions of a number of other secret bases, including an installation at Benecia, California, and an underground base that had been located in an old railroad tunnel at Ukiah, California, with the purpose of creating a base that was less vulnerable to nuclear attack.

The documents show that the base is part of the FEMA "COG" (Continuity of Government) plan, to preserve electronics communications and the continuance of government in the case of war or natural cataclysm, and to provide a safe haven for government officials, scientists, and others — everybody except the public — during times of national emergency. The documents note that the black choppers have been involved in provisioning the underground base.

When asked to comment on the base and the routine black chopper flights that come and go from it, the Air Force only admits that, "The helicopter traffic over the Napa hills is a classified operation." Officials from Hamilton Air Force Base, however, admit that the helicopters are flown from the base.

According to journalist Harry V. Martin, "The local media, despite receiving reports of such activities themselves, have attempted to make a farce out of the numerous reports..."

One newspaper, however, took the reports seriously. According to Martin, "The *Napa Sentinel* reported the flight patterns, interviewed eyewitnesses, talked to military and intelligence sources, and provided a scenario for the entire phenomenon. Since that period of time, however, reports have surfaced across the country. Black helicopters overhead, unmarked. In a few ground sightings, the occupants of the helicopters have been described as wearing black uniforms carrying automatic weapons..."

One source cited by Martin indicates that FEMA operates the black helicopters in conjunction with the Wackenhut Corporation. Wackenhut is a monolithic private security organization, founded by FBI alumnus George Wackenhut, and over the years staffed at an executive level by high level FBI, CIA and other former intelligence agency members. Current and recent members of the Wackenhut board of directors include former CIA Deputy Director Admiral Bobby Ray Inman, former FBI Director Clarence Kelley, former Defense Secretary and former CIA Deputy Director Frank Carlucci, former Defense Intelligence Agency Director General Joseph Carroll. [7]

One of Wackenhut's penchants is collecting files, building the largest privately-held collection of intelligence dossiers extant on politically incorrect American citizens. By 1966 Wackenhut could boast that they possessed files on four million Americans, but by now that figure may be chickenfeed.

According to insiders, Wackenhut enjoys that most special of special relationships with the government. Supplying security to U.S. embassies internationally, and guarding nearly all of the strategic facilities in the U.S., Wackenhut might just as well be considered as an arm of the government, a cut-out conveniently privatized to bypass oversight.

This view is echoed by intelligence agents past and present, at least those who are willing to talk. They describe a shake-up in the CIA after Senate Intelligence Committee revelations of wrongdoing, and a change of policy dictating that many of the most sensitive of intelligence operations would be performed privately. One former agent describes a written proposal from George Wackenhut to the CIA offering Wackenhut offices around the world to be used as fronts for CIA activity. [8]

William Corbett, a former CIA intelligence analyst, has said, "Wackenhut would allow the CIA to occupy positions within the company [in order to carry out] clandestine operations." [9]

Wackenhut's latest money-making venture has been into the private prison industry, which it has entered into in a big way. Wackenhut is currently the third largest private prison provider in the world, with a dozen or more facilities in the United States and Australia, and with plans to build other prisons in South America, Europe, and the Pacific Rim. As the world goes more dictatorial, these prisons will certainly not go begging. And Wackenhut's relatively new venture into private prisons neatly fits into the FEMA plan, for the primary "emergency" that federal authorities foresee in the future is not a volcano or seasonal flooding, but an uprising of one or more segments of the American populace. [10]

Counting down another hit in our "disturbing trends" list, hastening the creation of America as a police state, is civil asset forfeiture. This is the confiscation of property from persons accused — not necessarily convicted —of crimes. The American fascisti are already employing this justification country-wide, with thousands of Americans losing all of their property, cars, homes, boats, planes, and businesses, sometimes based only on the word of anonymous informants who have said that these persons have committed a crime.

Examples of these atrocities:

— In Detroit in December 1988, police raided a grocery store alleged to have been involved in the sale of drugs. Although no drugs were found on the premises, drug-sniffing canines reacted to three $100 bills taken from the case register, providing justification for the confiscation of $4,384 from the store. A report in the *Pittsburgh Press* states, however, that over 92% of all cash in circulation shows drug residue.

— In October of 1992, Trail's End, the five million dollar, 200-acre Malibu ranch of 61-year-old Donald Scott was raided by a multi-jurisdictional cop force of 31 persons. Members of the assault force included the Los Angeles County Sheriff's Department, the Drug Enforcement Agency, National Park Service Rangers, and California Bureau of Narcotic Enforcement personnel. As the police bashed in Scott's door, knocking his wife out of the way, the man appeared from his bedroom with a gun in hand. Told to lower his gun, he complied with the order, only to be shot dead by an over-zealous L.A. County Sheriff's Deputy.

It turned out that the entire justification for the jackbooted tactics employed on Scott was the testimony of a paid federal informant who thought he had seen, without binoculars, a marijuana plantation while flying 1,000 feet above the Scott property. At least one secret warrantless search had already been conducted on the property without turning up anything.

And after murdering Scott, the MJTF forces found that there was nary a pot seed to be found.

Marijuana was the justification for the raid on Donald Scott's property, but apparently not the actual reason this man was targeted. A five month investigation by the Ventura County District Attorney had noted that the National Park Service had previously made a number of cash offers to purchase Scott's property, which he had declined. Given asset forfeiture laws, Scott was set up so that the Sheriff's Department could confiscate the property, then sell it to the Park Service for an estimated five million dollars. Further proof that there was a monetary motive in the Scott case was that the sheriff's deputies had done a property appraisal ranch prior to the raid, and that asset forfeiture of the property was mentioned in a police briefing prior to kicking in the front door of the place. The deputies even noted on the appraisal the price of a comparable piece of property recently sold in the area.

Ventura County District Attorney Michael Bradbury has been critical of the actions of the MJTF team whose actions were responsible for the death of Donald Scott. He has said, "In short, this caper smells... distinctly acquisitory." [11]

— In 1992 a drug informant told the Department of Public Safety in Glendale, Arizona that 28-year-old Greg Rivera was engaged in marijuana smuggling. The informant was given $3,400 for the information. Rivera's house was raided on June 17, 1992, and the entirety of Rivera's assets were seized, including a pickup truck and a ski boat. Rivera was not even charged with a crime due to lack of evidence, but several years later his property had still not been returned.

— Currently asset forfeitures in America total at least four billion dollars per year, and the 1991 Omnibus Crime Bill has extended the amount of time that the authorities have to return assets which have been improperly seized, from six months to six and one-half years. Is there any doubt that America has evolved a homegrown Gestapo? [12]

— An area where asset forfeiture has turned into an octopus of incredible proportions is Louisiana. Witnesses have reported, as detailed on the *Dateline NBC* program of January 3, 1997, that police officers in that state are illegally stopping travelers and holding them at gun point while money, vehicles, and other possessions are confiscated. Those who protest the actions are put in jail. Monies and vehicles are then divided among the police, district attorneys, and judges taking part in the illegal actions.

Baton Rouge lawyer Jim Boren indicates, "There is no question that it is a statewide problem. You can't go to any parish in the state without talking to people who have horror stories about this sort of thing.

"The judges are afraid because they will be called 'soft on crime.' The state of Louisiana is aware of the abuses but no legislator has the courage to sponsor reform legislation for fear of being labeled as the spokesman of the dope dealers of America.

"A lot of innocent people get hassled and have to fight to get their own property back because we are afraid to reform the system."

After the airing of the *Dateline* program the Louisiana governor's office was inundated with over 1,000 messages from around the nation. This prompted Governor Mike Foster to hedge his bets by saying that he is "always willing to consider whether there are changes that need to be made in Louisiana laws to add additional protections, both for society as a whole and for those who may be treated unjustly." [13]

NOTES:

1. "The Houlihan Report," excerpted from *Taking Aim,* Volume 1, Number 5, 1994
2. Goldberg and Badhwar, "Blueprint for Tyranny," *Penthouse* magazine, undated essay
3. Ibid.
4. Blair, Mike, "Reserves' Command Structure Configured to Match FEMA," *The Spotlight,* November 7, 1994
5. Ibid.
6. Blair, Mike, "FEMA Takes Over Reserve Forces," *The Spotlight,* July 3, 1995

7. Martin, Harry V., "Black Helicopters: What Are They Doing in Napa?," "Media Scorn: Links with FEMA and Wackenhut Corporation," the *Napa Sentinal*, copies obtained from the Internet, 1995; Connolly, John, "Inside the Shadow CIA," *SPY* magazine, September 1992
8. Connolly
9. Ibid.
10. Millman, Joel, "Captive Market," *Forbes* magazine, September 16, 1991; "Wackenhut is Out to Prove That Crime Does Pay," *Business Week*, December 17, 1990.
11. "Asset Forfeiture, The Looting of America — and It's the Law?", *The Probe*, Fall, 1996; Arnold, Andrew, "America Under Siege," *The Spotlight*, March 17, 1997; Kanner, Gideon. "Never Mind, 'Only' Property Rights Were Violated," *The Wall Street Journal*, August 25, 1993
12. "Asset Forfeiture, The Looting of America — and It's the Law?"
13. *Dateline NBC* television, January 3, 1997; Blair, Mike, "Patriots Make Governor Cry 'Uncle,' *The Spotlight*, January 20, 1997

7

BIG BROTHER IS WATCHING YOU

An agency virtually unknown to the man in the street, one busily engaged in consolidating totalitarian control in America, is FinCEN. The Financial Crimes Enforcement Network was established on April 25, 1990 by Treasury Secretary Nicholas Brady. A FinCEN factsheet, disseminated by the Department of the Treasury, drolly records,

"The Treasury Department established FinCEN to collate, analyze, and disseminate information on financial crimes, especially drug money laundering." FinCEN's mission, according to the same factsheet, "is to provide a government-wide, multi-source intelligence and analytical network to support law enforcement and regulatory agencies in the detection, investigation, and prosecution of financial crimes."

Although FinCEN has only 200 employees, these are computer experts and intelligence analysts who actively liase with other agencies; thus FinCEN is a computerized overseer for financial crime and what the feds consider crime that has assimilated the networks of two dozen federal agencies, as well as American and foreign police agencies.

FinCEN issues over 10,000 reports a year, and freely accesses databases that include those of the IRS, the Secret Service, the FBI, The DEA, the Customs Service, the Census Bureau, the Postal Service, the CIA, the NSA, the DIA, the BATF, the INS, the NSC, the Federal Deposit Insurance Corporation, the Federal Reserve, the Comptroller of the Currency, and the State Department's Bureau of Intelligence and Research. FinCEN roams free through the databases of every state in the U.S., as well as dipping into the records of commercial information sources such as credit records, telephone bills, and even the receipts of purchases at supermarkets.

National boundaries do not provide a barrier to the long arm of FinCEN: the agency has data trading agreements with government and police worldwide, as for instance with the Nazi-compromised Interpol. [1]

One would think — or hope — that an individual would be lost in such an avalanche of paperwork and computerwork, but FinCEN brags about using what is called the "Artificial Intelligence/Massive Parallel Processing System," that mimics human thought to ferret out alleged offenders. Fine tuning these capabilities, FinCEN employees have also been put through training programs enabling them to mimic human thought.

Computer expert Clark Matthews reports that, "According to people who have dealt with FinCEN — as well as published accounts — the agency's computers are already busy gathering lifetime financial histories of all American citizens. They are identifying assets, tracking income and cash flows, checking credit histories, retirement accounts, pension plans, insurance records and more. Your assets are reportedly being indexed to your Social Security number, for future 'action' by authorities by the FBI, Drug Enforcement Agency, Internal Revenue Service, Treasury Department or local law enforcement." [2]

The Computer Professionals for Social Responsibility watchdog group ask some pointed questions about the significance of FinCEN:

"In what other ways might FinCEN's... skill in centralizing information — in matching, combining, comparing and linking facts in order to reveal hidden activities, to tell certain kinds of stories — be deployed? In what ways, for example, could [FinCEN] be turned against law-abiding citizens?

"...How [might] FinCEN serve a tyrannical successor regime, should it seize power in this country as a means of control? There is little question that this anti-drug tool could also serve as a potent instrument of repression."

One of the most incredible of FinCEN's ambitions is to put an American "Deposit Tracking System" in place, a program to track all of the monetary transactions taking place in U.S. bank and credit card accounts. This DTS system may have been approved by executive order even as this is written. [3]

At the same time that FinCEN hardwires surveillance and offers it up to the lords of control, the Internal Revenue Service is performing a similar service. In 1995 the IRS began an $8 billion dollar computer system upgrade, consolidating all of their databases into a super surveillance system containing detailed information on virtually every American — called Compliance 2000.

The *New York Post* informs us that, "In addition to detailing its plan, the IRS gave notice that 'this system is exempt from the notification, access and contest provisions of the Privacy Act (1974).' This means that the IRS doesn't need permission to dig up information, doesn't need to show it to you and doesn't need to correct the information even if it's wrong." [4]

Far from an agency with any ethical qualms, as most Americans realize, the IRS has long been a weapon for whatever governmental regime happens to be in power. Since last year, for example, the IRS has been launching financial audits against at least a dozen non-profit groups, activist groups, and individuals who are seen as part of a "right-wing conspiracy" lined up against the Clinton gang.

Among the groups who have come in for audits are the Heritage Foundation, the American Immigration Control Foundation, the Western Journalism Center, and the National Rifle Association. A survey conducted by the *Washington Times* was unable to locate any leftist or Clinton-friendly non-profit groups receiving similar scrutiny.

The Western Journalism Center was audited after the group was singled out in a White House "action plan" focused on countering publicity about wrongdoing amongst the members of the Clinton administration. Joseph Farah of the WJC notes that IRS examiners specifically requested documents "related to the selection of Christopher Ruddy as an investigative reporter and how the topic [of Whitewater] was selected." Ruddy is a reporter who has continued to pursue information relating to the suspicious death of Vince Foster.

The National Rifle Association came under IRS scrutiny one month after Clinton vocally blamed the group for tipping the scales in an election takeover of Congress by the Republicans. NRA spokespersons estimate that the audit is costing the group one million dollars per year, as thousands of internal documents are being pried forth, and NRA office space commandeered by IRS agents.

Among private individuals called to task by the IRS have been Kent Masterson Brown, the attorney who revealed Hillary Clinton's secret health care task force; an otherwise innocuous Chicago couple who made the mistake of openly criticizing President Clinton during a public forum; and Billy Dale, the former director of the White House Travel Office, who was axed by the First Lady. [5]

Newly fine-tuned human tracking capabilities are also being dialed-up worldwide. In 1993 the United States military began the use of what is termed the Deployable Mass Population Identification and Tracking System (DMPITS), using it first on 34,000 Haitian refugees being processed at Guantanamo naval base in Cuba. Since that time, the DMPITS system has been purchased by the U.S. Department of Immigration and Naturalization Service (INS), and has also been installed at border patrol stations in San Diego, California in 1994. DMPITS provides a taste of the kind of security measures that will no doubt soon be instituted on American citizens en masse.

After being hustled into the local security station, the subject to be scanned by the DMPITS cyclops is led to sit goggle-eyed in front of a console concealing a bank of computerized equipment. This includes a Hewlett-Packard 715 or 735 UNIX workstation with a 2 gigabyte internal hard drive, a color monitor, keyboard, mouse, fingerprint scanner, a tag scanner for programming and accessing a microchip-implanted plastic ID bracelet, and a color videocam. The system is backed up with a HP-735 workstation with 80m of RAM and a 525 GB external hard drive, with flatbed scanner, laser printer, and modem. The subject is then led — forced, if necessary — to place their right index finger on the red glowing surface of a Touchprint pad to be scanned by the Congent System for Automated Fingerprint Identification System (AFIS).

After fingerprints are taken, the subject is interrogated for a wide variety of information including name, sex, birthdate, family members, nationality, point of origin, medical history, distinguishing marks, associations, work history, school records, housing records, immunization records, and any number of other facts that surely cannot be anyone else's business than his own. This information is then instantly programmed into a microchip in an ID bracelet that is clamped onto the subject's wrist. The bracelet can later be scanned for up to 1,600 pages of information. [6]

Providing another deep, deep look into the affairs of virtually every citizen of this country is that innocuous creature, the telephone. Without any ado from the freedom watchdogs at NBC and others, the Clinton administration has ordered U.S. telephone companies to install electronic wiretap capability in all telephones manufactured in the United States, and backup monitoring equipment to access it, by October 28, 1998.

It must be obvious to even the most deluded of administration apologists that tapping telephones without prior warrant is a violation of anti-wiretapping laws, as well as the Fourth Amendment to the Constitution, which states that "The right of the people to be secure in their persons, houses, papers, and effects, against unreasonable searches and seizures, shall not be violated." [7]

The justification of this blatant disregard of constitutional rights is the 1994 Communications Assistance for Law Enforcement Act (CALEA), also known as the "Wiretap Access Bill." The "Capacity Requirements" listed in this bill stipulate a minimum of 540,000 and a maximum of 1.5 million telephone "intercepts" to take place at any particular time by American intelligence agencies, although in practice this will surely translate to unlimited access.

Not only do these intercepts provide access to the audio

content of phone calls, but they also monitor and record telephone numbers called, cross referencing them to the records of who and when you call, pick up the content of faxes, and record the content of computer transmissions. [8]

Another major step by Big Brother in monitoring the American populace, ushered in as usual by the back door, is the aptly-named Illegal Immigration Reform and Immigrant Responsibility Act of 1996. This bill was signed into law in September of 1996 by President Clinton. If you didn't thoroughly read through the hundreds of pages of the bill (and I doubt that many of the hackpols who voted on it did) then you will not have gotten to the juicy parts, starting on page 650, and you will not have noticed that Congress has approved a national ID card.

Portions of the bill lock together in an insidious jigsaw puzzle with an Orwellian pay-off. In Sections 401-403, pilot programs are mandated to be put into action, including the "Machine Readable Document Pilot Program."

This program directs that employers must obtain a computerized document reader that is to be placed on-line with the Social Security Administration, in order to scan a national ID card of all prospective employees. After the Social Security department receives the information transmitted by the employer, it has the option to approve or disapprove the hiring by the employer, or to institute other actions against the person seeking a job.

Section 656 of the law says that, "after October 1, 2000, Federal agencies may only accept as proof of identity driver's licenses that conform to standards developed by the Secretary of the Treasury," determined by consultation with officials of state motor vehicle bureaus and the American Association of Motor Vehicle Administrators. We already know what the AAMVA wants in terms of identification: digital fingerprints and other information, probably of the DMPITS variety.

Earlier Senate hearings on "Verification of Applicant Identity for the Purposes of Employment and Public Assistance," held on May 10, 1995, define the types of information that will be required. Robert Razor of the Secret Service Financial Crimes Division of the FBI said at the hearings, "The use of biometrics is the means by which an individual may be conclusively identified. There are two types of biometric identifiers: physical and behavioral characteristics. Physiological biometrics include facial features, hand geometry, retinal and iris patterns, DNA, and fingerprints. Behavioral characteristics include voice characteristics and signature analysis."

During the Senate hearings Dianne Feinstein made clear her intention to support the national ID card, that would include a "magnetic strip on it which the bearer's unique voice, retina pattern, or fingerprint is digitally encoded." She offered an aside that, "fifteen years ago they would have torn the building down." Senator Alan Simpson repeated the sentiment at the close of the subcommittee meeting:

"There is much to do here, but I was just saying to Ted [Kennedy] before he left, a hearing like this fifteen years ago, would have torn the building down. And here we are today, just a bunch of us, kind of sitting around and no media, no nothing. This is fine with me. I get tired of them on this issue." [9]

Lest you think I am cooking the data to make the situation seem worse than it is, the following fax was received by a patriot newsletter: "A friend of mine showed me a letter she received yesterday from the Illinois Department of Public Aid, it requires all people who receive Aid for Dependent Children to accept biometric identification or lose their assistance. I know you might think that I'm making this up so I have attached three images that I scanned which is the entire letter." [10]

The information in this chapter is the tip of the iceberg in terms of government's attempts to digitize your soul. And with each year Big Brother's technological capability increases, as data files are cross referenced, as your conversations and computers are monitored, as financial dealings are scrutinized, and as total control is brought on-line by increments.

Big Brother is watching you.

NOTES:

1. Meldal-Johnson and Young. *The Interpol Connection.* Dial Press, New York, 1979
2. Matthews, Clark, "Technology & Liberty," *The Spotlight,* January 24, 1994
3. McAlvany, Donald S., "Privacy Abolished: The U.S. Financial Surveillance Juggernaut," *The McAlvany Intelligence Advisor,* December 1995
4. McAlvany; "Revealed: IRS Is Tracking You In Cyberspace," *New York Post,* October 16, 1995
5. "IRS Audits Clinton's Critics," *Middle American News,* March 1997
6. Braxeman, Lynne, *Automatic I.D. News,* December 1994
7. McAlvany, Donald S., "Privacy Abolished: The U.S. Financial Surveillance Juggernaut," *The McAlvany Intelligence Advisor,* December, 1995; Department of Treasury factsheet on FinCEN, November 26, 1995
8. Matthews, Clark, "Million Wiretaps Planned," *The Spotlight,* November 13, 1995
9. Parker, Cyndee, "National ID Card Is Now Federal Law and Georgia Wants to Help Lead the Way." Obtained on the Internet
10. Grapevine Publishing, Boise, Idaho, March 1997

8

POLICE STATE CHRONOLOGY

The following is a brief update on the encroachments of Police State America to date. This chronology is far from complete, since significant events can be gleaned from the newspapers and from the screams of your neighbors almost every day.

1994

— In the early part of 1994, the Bureau of Alcohol, Tobacco and Firearms (BATF), involved in such debacles as Waco and Ruby Ridge, received a budget increase during a period when other government agencies were experiencing extreme cuts. Radio Free America reports that a dozen military attack jets were given to the BATF at this time. [1]

— On June 3, 1994, President Clinton signed Executive Order 12919, dubbed "National Defense Industrial Preparedness," yet another ED bolstering the power of the executive office, and moving the country closer to being a dictatorship, given broadly defined conditions of national emergency. [2]

— In June of 1994, a 12-day training exercise dubbed "Grecian Firebolt '94" was held at Fort Indiantown Gap, Pennsylvania, involving approximately 10,000 U.S. military personnel. During this exercise the military was engaged in communications exercises with FEMA. Fort Indiantown Gap is one of several locations intended as a detention camp for dissidents or others during a national crisis. [3]

— July 1994: "A Multi-Jurisdictional Task Force assault team consisting of FBI agents and 300 Marines from the 22nd Marine Expeditionary Unit at Camp Lejeune, North Carolina, conducted an anti-terrorist night raid with black helicopters on Tybee Island, near Savannah, Georgia." [4]

— According to a report dated September 16, 1994, a barber in Sandpoint, Idaho was talking with an Alaskan state trooper on vacation, getting his hair cut. The trooper mentioned the warrantless search-and-seizure programs verifiably taking place throughout Alaska. When the barber asked if the Alaskan troopers had probable cause when they approached the door of citizens, the man responded, "Well, sometimes we do and sometimes we don't." According to the trooper, it didn't make much difference.

Probing the trooper for answers, the barber asked him what type of questions they asked the people who opened their doors. The trooper said that they first inquired whether there was anything illegal in the home. If so, what?

If the resident responded by saying that there was nothing illegal inside, the troopers then asked if it was all right for them to enter and search the home. If the residents refused the search, they were seen as suspicious and threatened with an investigation.

According to the trooper, three out of four persons allowed a search of their homes. [5]

— In September of 1994, information was released by Special Forces and other operatives charging that the Delta Force, the counter-terrorist force that works out of Langley Air Force Base, had its charter changed to include domestic operations against Americans. Later reports, in 1995, suggested that both the Delta Force and the Navy SEALS had been surveyed by the Justice Department about their willingness to participate in Justice and Treasury raids on Americans. [6]

— Beginning in October, Detroit was turned into a war zone by clashes between local gangs and black clad, ninja-style multi-jurisdictional task forces armed with machine guns and short shotguns. These task forces were reportedly composed of FBI, BATF, IRS and other federal agencies, along with local and state police. On November 11, 100 agents and a street gang engaged in a shoot-out in the Cass Corridor on Detroit's east side. During the melee, an ambulance and a Department of Public Works step van were commandeered by the MJTF agents, who refused to identify themselves when asked on what authority they were taking the vehicles. [7]

— In October, 1994, the FBI established what they call an anti-terrorist training center in Belle Chasse, Louisiana, a suburb of New Orleans. The site, however, is a milti-jurisdictional task force facility, since doors are marked for the FBI, National Security Council, Drug Enforcement Agency, and other agencies. One of the first activities taking place at the facility, in the month of its opening, was an exercise involving 1,000 federal agents and other employees.

A media tour was provided for part of the FBI complex, but according to the *Times Picayune,* "civilians were closely watched and were required to reveal their Social Security numbers before gaining access... As they entered offices, workers promptly shut down laptop computers and cleared their screens for alleged security reasons..." [8]

— In 1994, BATF agents closed in on the home of Monique Montgomery at four in the morning. As they burst through a door, Montgomery reached for a gun and was shot and killed by the agents. Nothing illegal was found in the home. [9]

1995

— On February 9, 1995, in West Hill, California, nine blocks in a residential area were sealed off by the Los Angeles Police Department. Thirty-five black and white police cruisers, Harbor Patrol units, and dogs were used in the operation. An officer who was asked the purpose of the operation said, "We are doing a training exercise for search and seizure of homes." When the exercise was completed a black Huey helicopter flew over the area. [10]

Other search and seizure programs were active about the same time as the California program. *The Christian Science Monitor* effuses, "The year-old program [of search and seizure] is credited with helping to achieve last year's record seizure of nearly 4,000 guns in St. Louis. More than 400 firearms were confiscated in 1994, after parents signed consent-to-search forms. Now the idea is spreading. San Diego and Pasadena, California have established their own consent-to-search programs. At least 25 other cities have expressed interest." [11]

— John M. Lekan, 54, a disabled chemical engineer, his wife Beverly, 49, and their son, John Jr., 9, lived in Brunswick, Ohio. Mrs. Lekan has multiple sclerosis and was receiving care from health aides of the Medina County Human Services Department. Lekan was informed that health aides had filed a complaint regarding the location of firearms in a house with a child. Lekan possessed a 10 gauge shotgun and a .27 caliber rifle.

On March 31, 1995, Brunswick policeman Sam Puzella knocked on Lekan's door. Refused entry, Puzella kicked the door in. Lekan shot Puzella. That evening Brunswick police rushed the home and Lekan shot two more of them. The neighborhood was evacuated, with gas, electric, and water shut off from the Lekans.

300 police officers, 200 fire fighters, and two armored personnel carriers converged on the home. Lekan and his son retreated into the basement, and firehoses were put in place to flood the area. 1,000 gallons a minute of water was pumped into the basement. The police broke through the garage door, and tear gas was fired.

Lekan and his son died, based upon statements of the police, by Lekan's hand. It was only later that the Brunswick Police Department admitted that Puzella, the officer who had initially broken down Lekan's door, did not have a search warrant. Two of Lekan's neighbors also mention that they have received phone calls threatening them to be quiet about what they saw during the siege. [12]

— In the morning, prior to the bombing of the Murrah Federal Building in Oklahoma City, Oklahoma, witnesses report that there were one or more black helicopters flying in the vicinity of the building.

A retired Joint Chiefs of Staff intelligence staff member also reports, "Be advised the night of the OKC bombing [April 19] that this FEMA base [Peter's Mountain, in Cismont, VA], and probably all other FEMA bases, had 'hot and cold running' choppers all night long! They used the OKC bombing as a 'catalytic' event to kick off a test of the Continuity of Government plan [COG]." [13]

— Beginning on April 24, 1995, Fort Indiantown Gap, 20 miles east of Harrisburg, Pennsylvania went into high gear with training of FBI, DEA and possibly other agencies for "heavy" assault training, using choppers and live firing exercises. Present was an FBI-converted motorhome with video equipment and electronics gear, including a 25-foot mast with videocam unit. A few weeks prior, Germans and Lithuanian military were observed on and around the base. [14]

— According to the military magazine *Aide-De-Camp,* "The Pentagon is considering changes in legislation to give the military the ability to be used in law enforcement situations in the U.S. in the event of nuclear, chemical or biological weapons usage." [15]

— In Key Largo, Florida, beloved of Bogey junkies, on June 22, 1995, at 11:50 p.m., residents were awoken by military exercises involving about 500 soldiers from Dade Collier Airport, Homestead Air Force Base, and Cape Canaveral Air Station. Black aircraft and helicopters attacked an environmentally protected area of the island with bullets and explosives. Area resident Meredith Cline says, "I don't have a problem with them conducting their simulation, but I do have problems with the length of it and the havoc they were causing down there." [16]

1996

— "The ATF have been stopping and searching vehicles on Highway 27 at Moore Haven, Florida off and on for the last two weeks. They wear full black uniforms and use a van to carry six-eight people and a dog." [17]

— On July 1, 1996, twelve individuals allegedly in the militia movement in Phoenix, Arizona were arrested. The media informed the public that they were members of the "Viper

Militia," and President Clinton was soon on the air wringing his hands and saying that their arrest had headed off "a terrible terrorist attack."

Upon further investigation, it was determined that one or more Bureau of Alcohol, Tobacco and Firearms agent provocateurs had infiltrated and become members of the group, and had encouraged the other members to perform criminal acts including the robbing of banks — encouragement that they rejected.

According to *Paranoia* Magazine, the indictment of the Viper Militia "refers not to a bombing conspiracy, but merely a 'Conspiracy to Furnish Instructions in the Use of Explosive Devices and Other Techniques...' It also refers to the Vipers' alleged 'teaching and demonstrating' of various firearm and explosive techniques. However, most of the weaponry, seized from the Viper Militia was apparently legal, as would be the teaching and demonstrating of its use. And all the magazines, books and videos possessed by the group were legal and constitutionally protected. Preventing attacks against innocent people is a laudable goal, but in this case the Feds seem to have manufactured most of the Vipers' venom." [18]

— The following is reprinted from the *Palatka Florida Daily News,* for October 7, 1996: "Beginning today police will be stopping motorists along certain public highways to ask them a few questions about where they are going and why, the Florida Department of Transportation stated. The 'Origin and Destination Surveys' will be conducted today through Thursday 'as part of the long term planning process,' said DOT spokeswoman Gina Bussher of DOT's Lake City office."

— The following, a poignant anonymous message from a police officer, was posted on the Internet in December of 1996:

> I'm a police officer on the East Coast. I can tell you for sure that a lot of local officers have recently been deputized as federal agents to work with ATF to grab guns. One of my best buddies is one of them. He advised that they are doing full traces on every gun they get their hands on, so make sure anything you have is 100% legal from day one. Their theory is that drugs and guns go together,

and gun convictions are much easier and cleaner, with sentences that start at 27 months.

They are especially hitting probationers and parolees. The other big thing is 'straw' purchases. In summary, there is a gun grab on, but they seem to be mostly interested in the druggies (at least here in the mid-Atlantic states).

The second thing I wanted to share with you was a little item left in my police department mailbox on 12-13-96. It's a copy of a teletype from the ATF to all state and local law enforcement agencies. The subject line is 'Enactment Omnibus Consolidated Appropriations Act of 1997' and advises agencies that anyone ever convicted of a misdemeanor relating to domestic violence must immediately give up all weapons and ammunition, both personal and issued.

Now they're taking guns from the cops, too! I swore to God that I would uphold the Constitution, but for the life of me I can't figure out how this could possibly be constitutional. Giving up a civil right for a misdemeanor conviction?

If you want to see a real jellyfish of a husband and father, come on over to my house and watch. I give up. I've already had Child Protective Services at my house on a Friday night because I had allegedly 'scared' my 15-year old daughter by yelling at her. They advised me they 'would have to take her out of the house.' Needless to say, they went nowhere with my daughter that night. Mind you, there was NO allegation of anything physical (It seems she heard at school that CPS would probably let her go live with her boyfriend and his mother).

I give up. They're going too far. I really don't think the police are out of hand, because I can still sleep with my conscience and am as fair as I think is possible, and I really believe my cohorts are generally just as fair minded. But all of these social agencies and the feds that back them are absolutely outrageous. Somebody wake me up. [19]

— The Bureau of Land Management proposed on December 5, 1996 to "stop vehicles; search any person, place or vehicle without warrant or process; seize without warrant or process any piece of evidence; and make arrests without warrant or process" on land held privately but next to or on bodies of water upstream from BLM land. [20]

1997

— March, 1997, *USA Today,* in a story titled "War Zone": "Charlotte, N.C. Mayor Pat McCrory said the Defense Department has agreed not to hold any more military training sessions in the city after an exercise Tuesday night surprised and scared some residents. About 100 soldiers participated in the urban exercise, accompanied by sounds of rocket fire and b   blasts, in a downtown warehouse district. 'My floors were vibrating, it was so loud,' said Kathleen O'Brien. Fort Bragg officials had notified the city a few months earlier, McCrory said. He said residents were supposed to be informed before the drill took place.

'One of the helicopters was so low, you could actually see this man inside and guns hanging outside of it,' stated Shannon Dugan, a waitress. 'We thought, what? Are we getting invaded?'"

The *Charlotte Observer* provided more detail on the "mock invasion." That source reported that the mayor of Charlotte announced that the Army had misled him about the proposed training when he met with them in December. Dennis Nowicki, Charlotte's police chief, also complained that he had not been told anything about the invasion by black helicopters until just a few hours before it took place. Other officials of the city were likewise adamant that they had been told nothing at all about the drill.

"The city got hoodooed..." said City Council member Malachi Greene. "These guys were not truthful. They lied by omission." [21]

— A patriot newsletter reports, "A 'constitutional' law enforcement officer has advised that the FBI/DOJ issued an 'all points alert' warning to law enforcement agencies to be on the alert for 'the true believers,' i.e., 'patriots' and their 'Revolution 2000' plan to overthrow the government."

The newsletter also noted, "Black Armored Vehicles: On the March 7, 1997, at 9:00 a.m., 94.7 radio had cell callers reporting 'two black tanks' on the Capitol Beltway (I-495) in Virginia... Furthermore, concurrently at 9:20 a.m., 'two black armored cars' were reported southbound on U.S. 29 about 8 miles south of Culpepper, Virginia." [22]

— In Knoxville, Tennessee, on April 3, 1997 a local man was conducting business at county offices with a friend. He noticed two Federal Police officers there, one of whom was known to him and who had at one time been with the Knoxville Police Department. The other man appeared to be a bodyguard, dressed in a black uniform with federal insignia. Curious, the man asked the officer about the federalization program, and was informed that "the Tennessee Valley Authority has always been a federal program."

Upon an inquiry about foreign troops being trained in the Smoky Mountains, the uniformed officer asked, "How did you know about that?" The federales immediately terminated the conversation and walked away.

The same source offers this information: "FYI... Federal Police cars are all around Knoxville and Knox County. Why, I wonder... This is not on TVA property." [23]

NOTES:

1. *World News Digest,* March 30, 1994
2. "Police State Activities in America," *The Patriot Report,* September 1995
3. Blair, Mike, *The Spotlight,* August 1, 1994
4. "Police State Activities in America"
5. Intel. Report, Militia of Montana, September 16, 1994
6. Rense, Jeff, "Delta Force Being Turned On Unsuspecting Americans?" *Contact* magazine, September 20, 1994; "Delta, Seals, Asked to Help Confiscate Civilian Arms," *The Resister,* Vol.1, No.1, November 25, 1995
7. Blair, Mike, "Detroit Turned into War Zone by Lawless, Lawmen," *The Spotlight,* December 5, 1994
8. "Feds Training to SWAT Enemies," *The Spotlight,* November 21, 1994
9. Arnold, Andrew, "America Under Siege," *The Spotlight,* March 17, 1997
10. "Updates from Southern California," *Silver State II* newsletter, February 19, 1995

11. Walters, Laurel Shaper, *Christian Science Monitor,* April 18, 1995
12. Information Packet, Militia of Montana, undated
13. Anonymous former Joint Chiefs of Staff source, April 23, 1997
14. Blair, Mike, "Feds Prepare for Heavy Assaults," *The Spotlight,* June 19, 1995
15. "Law Enforcement Role Sought for Military in U.S.," *The Patriot Report,* November 1995
16. Blair, Mike, "Multi-Jurisdictional Force Terrorizes Rural Floridians," *The Spotlight,* August 7, 1995
17. "Letters to the Editor," *The Patriot Report,* May 1996
18. "The Real Vipers," *Paranoia* magazine, Winter 1996/1997
19. Anonymous Internet posting, December 14, 1996
20. Arnold
21. "War Zone," *USA Today,* March 6, 1997; Hechinger, Perlmutt, Price, "The 'Invasion' of Third Ward," The *Charlotte Observer, March 6, 1997*
22. Patriotic Citizen/Remnant Alert for Period March 3-7, 1997
23. Internet posting on April 3, 1997

9

NEW WORLD INVASION

B lack helicopters and the transition to an American police state are only fully understood in a broader context: the New World Order. Since August 1990, when President Bush let the rat out of the bag by announcing the birth of a New World Order (the plot had actually been in progress for decades prior to the announcement), there has been an accelerating violation of constitutional safeguards and the destruction of U.S. sovereignty.

Although the final stages of the consolidation of the New World Order are currently taking place worldwide, this conspiracy was spawned many years ago amongst elitists hungry for total world control. Conceived as early as the 1700s, carried forward by a host of super-secret organizations like the Illuminati, the Rhodes Round Table, and the Skull and Bones society, and merely secretive ones such as the Bilderbergers, the Trilateral Commission, and The Council on Foreign Relations, the plan has been to destroy national sovereignties worldwide and to globalize government in an unelected dictatorship of the rich. Judging from their literature, the current generation of power mongers see the common man as fodder for their plans, and America, where a tradition of liberty has existed since its inception as a nation, as nothing more than an obstacle to their ambitions.

As early as January of 1954, the U.S. Congress studied resolutions proposing the surrender of American sovereignty to the U.N.. Originating from the subcommittee on the United Nations Charter, a document titled "Review of the United Nations Charter" proposes the following:

"This resolution declares the sense of Congress that a

fundamental objective of the United States foreign policy should be (1) to support and strengthen the United Nations, and (2) to seek its development into a world federation... with... powers adequate to preserve peace... and enforcement of world law."

The document also records that, "Mr. Cord Meyer, chairman of the National Executive committee of the United World Federalists, gave the following views to the committee: By passing this resolution we in the United States would be declaring our willingness to join with other nations in transferring to the U.N., constitutional authority to administer and enforce law that was finding on national governments and their individual citizens."

Finally, most clearly, "Supranational government is the only way to end war and the threat of war. State sovereignty must be curbed. This resolution is the first step in the direction of creating world government..." [1]

Echoing this theme of "supranational government" was a study commissioned by the State Department in February, 1961. The Institute for Defense Analyses prepared Study Memorandum No. 7, "A World Effectively Controlled by the United Nations," penned by the Council on Foreign Relations' Lincoln P. Bloomfield.

Bloomfield doesn't pull any punches when he tells us, in the opening paragraph of the document, "A world effectively controlled by the United Nations is one in which 'world government' would come about through the establishment of supranational institutions, characterized by mandatory universal membership and some ability to employ physical force. Effective control would thus entail a preponderance of political power in the hands of a supranational organization..."

Bloomfield saw as necessary to the institution of world government:

(1) powers sufficient to monitor and enforce disarmament, settle disputes, and keep the peace — including taxing powers...

(2) an international force, balanced appropriately among ground, sea, air, and space elements, consisting of 500,000 men, recruited individually, wearing a U.N. uniform, and controlling a

nuclear force composed of 50-100 mixed land-based mobile and undersea-based missiles, averaging one megaton per weapon;
(3) governmental powers distributed among three branches...
(4) compulsory jurisdiction of the International Court..."

Clarifying what he meant in surprisingly candid fashion, Bloomfield defined his terms: "'World' means that the system is global, with no exceptions to its fiat: universal membership. 'Effectively controlled' connotes... a relative monopoly of physical force at the center of the system, and thus a preponderance of political power in the hands of a supranational organization... 'The United Nations' is not necessarily precisely the organization as it now exists... Finally, to avoid endless euphemism and evasive verbiage, the contemplated regime will occasionally be referred to unblushingly as a 'world government.'" [2]

Further perspective on what has been going on in this country may be obtained by consulting State Department Publication 7277, also drafted in 1961. This document clearly explains foreign troops are being billeted within the United States, while at the same time there is a dispersion of our own forces into myriad foreign hotspots, and a convergence and joint training of our troops with foreign troops worldwide. 7277 also explains why American soldiers are now being commanded by United Nations officers, and why large amounts of Russian military equipment is being imported into the United States.

According to 7277, "The revolutionary development of modern weapons within a world divided by serious ideological differences has produced a crisis in human history. In order to overcome the danger of nuclear war now confronting mankind, the United States has introduced at the Sixteenth General Assembly of the United Nations a Program for General and Complete Disarmament in a Peaceful World.

"This new program provides for the progressive reduction of the war-making capabilities of nations and the simultaneous strengthening of international institutions to settle disputes and maintain the peace."

"...The overall goal of the United States is a free, secure, and peaceful world of independent states adhering to common standards of justice and international conduct and subjecting the use of force to the rule of law; a world which has achieved general and complete disarmament under effective international control; and a world in which adjustment to change takes place in accordance with the principles of the United Nations.

Also stipulated in Publication 7277 are the objectives to which nations should direct their efforts, including: "The disbanding of all national armed forces," and "the elimination from national arsenals of all armaments," "the establishment and effective operation of an international Disarmament Organization within the framework of the United Nations."

Publication 7277 details a three-stage operation:

Stage One: Disarmament begins with treaties and joint access agreements, as well as the utilization of unarmed peacekeeping operations by the U.N. This stage is completed.

Stage Two: At this point, a 'permanent international peace force within the United Nations' is constructed, a peace force which will be 'progressively strengthened.' Also called for is 'The dismantling or the conversion to peaceful uses of certain military bases and facilities wherever located.' This step is currently in progress — official sources indicate that the U.S. Army has closed over 350 bases worldwide.

Stage Three: When stage two is completed, a point is aimed for when 'no state would have the military power to challenge the progressively strengthened U.N. peace force.' [3]

Clarification on the progress of the U.S. toward the goals outlined in Publication 7277 is a "Statement on the Posture of the United States Army FY 95," released in February, 1994. Quoting the document:

> The Army has accomplished all of these missions and more, while at the same time inactivating and restationing units, releasing soldiers and civilians (over 408,000 since 1989), reducing its overall budget, promulgating a new fighting doctrine... The Army has become smaller than at any time since the beginning of the Cold

War, while also being called upon to carry out an increasing number of missions around the world...

The Army is in its ninth year of steady resource decline, with more reductions to come. This already is one of the longest periods of negative real growth since before World War II. The initial draw down strategy of trading force structure for readiness has run its course.

States would retain only those forces, non-nuclear armaments, and establishments required for the purpose of maintaining internal order; they would also support and provide agreed manpower for a U.N. Peace Force.

Beginning in the early 1990s the long term plans of the internationalists went into overdrive. No longer were they observing the rule of the Socialist Fabian Society to "Proceed Slowly"; now they were in a breakneck drive for the creation of the New World Order by the year 2001. Signs of the New World Order were suddenly everywhere:

The U.N. suddenly became more broadly interventionist, with ongoing operations, or planned operations including, in a survey compiled by the CIA: Abkhazia, Angola, Bosnia-Hercegovina, Cambodia, Croatia, Cyprus, El Salvador, Eritrea [Ethiopia], the Golan Heights, Haiti, Jerusalem, Kashmir, Kuwait, Lebanon, Liberia, Moldova, Mozambique, Nagorno-Karabakh, Rwanda, Sinai, the Solomon Islands, Somalia, South Africa, South Ossetia [Georgia], Sri Lanka, Sudan, Tajikistan, Western and the Sahara. [4]

In December 1992 George Bush launched a "humanitarian mission," ordering 30,000 U.S. troops to Somalia without congressional authorization. His pretext was a U.N. resolution — that he had requested be enacted. President Clinton shortly upped the ante, turning the "humanitarian mission" into a major military foray.

On October 3, 1993, Clinton placed 4,000 U.S. soldiers under the command of Turkish General Cevik Bir, in the service of the U.N., the first time that American troops had ever been placed under foreign command. [5]

One means for a smooth transition to a world army and the

discarding of American sovereignty, involves the melding of the American military and the fighting forces of other countries.

The Chairman of the Joint Chiefs of Staff, General John Salikashvili, was the person who came up with that bright notion called "Bridge to America," and another called "Partnership for Peace," that authorize sending American National Guard, Army Reserve, and other Reserve personnel to countries in the former USSR, as well as to shuttle troops from these former Soviet countries to America to take part in exercises.

According to a working paper published by the National Guard Bureau on June 24, 1994, for "...the past year and a half, the National Guard Bureau has worked with the Joint Staff and the U.S. European Command to establish National Guard State Partnerships linking National Guards of selected U.S. States with Ministries of Defense throughout Central and Eastern Europe (CEE) and Newly Independent States (NIS) of the former Independent States (NIS) of the former Soviet Union. The Partnerships assist the participating nations' transition to democratic military institutions with peacetime utility in providing military support of civilian authorities."

Not only have American troops been melded with troops of the Eastern Bloc, but they have been assisting the former Soviet bloc countries in enforcing martial law.

The working paper goes on to say, "Contingent on receiving proper funding, the National Guard is anxious to extend the State Partnership, such an offer is both appropriate and timely. Such action would support the President's Partnership for Peace program and be an example of on-going bilateral success that could be emulated by our NATO allies. Such an offer also would demonstrate to the Russians that participation in the Partnership for Peace is inclusive vice exclusive. Acceptance would involve them directly with Heartland America..."

Insanely, incredibly, overseeing a national task force on U.S. military base closures, is Mikhail Gorbachev. Far from being a hippie with the mark of the beast who just happened to walk upon the world stage, Gorbachev was carefully groomed to assume power in the Soviet Union by his hardline KGB mentor, Yuri Andropov.

In late April, 1993 Mikhail Gorbachev and his Gorbachev Foundation USA moved into their new headquarters, a white-shingled bayfront house at the historic Presidio military base in San Francisco. The Gorbachev Foundation obtains funding from outfits like the Rockefellers Brothers Fund, the Mellon Foundation, the Ford Foundation, and the Pew Family Trusts, all of which have set up long-term endowments.

The Gorbachev Foundation is run by Dr. James A. Garrison, formerly with the Esalen Institute at Big Sur, in California. Esalen is the grandaddy of the touchy-feely metaphysical institutes, and has been promoting New Age gurus and seminars since the 1960s. Garrison and his ilk (like Bill and Hillary Clinton) no doubt see turning the world into one big Love-in as the answer to American-Russian animosities. But does Gorbachev?

Speaking in San Francisco, Gorbachev indicated that the foundation was creating a national task force on U.S. military base closings. "California," Gorbachev said, "is already a pioneer of conversion." He stressed that the process isn't painless and required a new form of thinking, "a conversion of the mind." Is there anyone out there, even Henry Kissinger, who doubts that that "conversion" would be to Marxism? [6]

A vital strategy for creating the New World Order, one also headed up by Gorbachev, is "Green Cross," a group that liases with the U.N. and UNESCO in its lofty ambitions to preserve the world environment. Gorbachev has sweepingly declared that, "The Green Cross is in its infancy but is already drawing strong support... We need a global focus... We have to change our values. We have to educate people... Educational systems all over the world must take up this task, international codes of law must be developed, and the practical work of environmental cleanup must be undertaken...

"Leaders in religion, politics and science must speak out and point us in new directions, toward a new paradigm for our civilization... If we're going to protect the planet's ecology, we're going to need to find alternatives to the consumerist [read Capitalist] dream that is attracting the world... We recognize the gradualness of change, as we recognize the urgency of change... We recognize that we will learn as we go. There is no clear answer, except that the old ideologies in our civilization must give way to the new challenges to our civilization. The growing environmental movement in the world must be the vehicle for that." [7]

Lauding Gorbachev, *New York Times* senior columnist Flora Lewis said, "Moscow's new idea... goes beyond accepted notions of the limits of national sovereignty and rules of behavior. It would seem to have an aspect of world government, because it would provide for the World Court to judge states... This is a breathtaking idea, beyond the current dreams of the ecology militants... And it is fitting that the environment be the topic for what amounts to global policing." [8]

OK: Ecology good, two legs bad. Why do I have the suspicion that, whales and spotted owls aside, Gorbachev is setting America up for the biggest fall of all? The Green Cross scheme, ostensibly intended to deal with environmental crises, was conceived while Gorbachev was still president of the Soviet Union and, in its literature and other public statements, it is apparent that its motivating creed is not the protection of chlorophyll, but the implementation of Communism in the guise of the New World Order.

Carl Bloice, a ranking American Communist with close ties to Gorbachev, has been so candid as to state, "the environmental movement promises to bring greater numbers into our orbit than the peace movement ever did."

One of the seminal documents informing Green Cross, is Agenda 21, adopted by the 1992 U.N. Earth Summit in Rio de Janeiro, and signed by the U.S. and other participating nations at the Summit. Agenda 21 has been described as a 'soft' law instrument, which commits signatory nations to shape their own laws and legislation in reflection of this overarching rag.

In the abridged version of the above text it is stated that, "Effective execution of Agenda 21 will require a profound reorientation of all human society, unlike anything the world has ever experienced — a major shift in the priorities of both governments and individuals and an unprecedented redeployment of human and financial resources. This shift will demand that a concern for the environmental consequences of every human action be integrated into individual and collective decision-making at every level.''

Everyone on Earth is included in the Agenda 21 plan...

"There are specific actions which are intended to be undertaken by multinational corporations and entrepreneurs, by financial institutions and individual investors, by high-tech companies and indigenous people, by workers and labor unions, by farmers and consumers, by students and schools, by government and legislators, by scientists, by women, by children — in short by every person on Earth.''

Commenting on the Agenda 21 document, *New York Times* writer William K. Stevens noted that the "soft laws" adopted by the Rio Earth Summit "have hidden teeth that will develop in the right circumstances." Stevens may feel that this is a positive thing. [9]

Another presiding spirit over the "greening" of the planet is Canadian oil magnate Maurice Strong, the first executive director of the U.N. Environmental Programme, director of the World Future Society, the founder of Planetary Citizens, founder of the World Economic Forum, trustee of the Rockefeller Foundation and the Aspen Institute, member of the Club of Rome, and a member of the U.N. Commission on Global Governance.

As reported in an Associated Press release of March 12, 1992, Strong said "...that the United States is the greatest threat to the world's ecological health." Strong said, "In effect, the United States is committing environmental aggression against the rest of the world.''

Strong is pushing for the creation of another layering of the global government infrastructure that masquerades under ecological concerns. If you would listen to Strong and a horde of deluded eco-freaks, we must save the earth by allowing the

Rockefellers and their social stratum to more thoroughly control it. So far they have been successful in implementing that goal. Every day that control is increasing. [10]

According to Cable New Network, a meeting took place on March 1, 1997, at Murray College in Kentucky. The matter which was discussed was the depopulation of two million acres in Kentucky and Tennessee, and the movement of half a million people in 17 counties in those two states. Scheduled was a special congressional committee that would examine the claims of ecologists on why this drastic measure must be implemented.

The measure that shaped the proposed massive movement of population was the Biological Diversity Treaty, a 20-page document hammered out at the Earth Summit in Rio de Janeiro in 1992. *Nexus* magazine reports upon the treaty: "In Article 25 there was to be a Global Biodiversity Assessment (GBA). This document of many thousands of pages outlines the plans to change the world. In the GBA, the following is stated:

"...Human beings are merely one strand in nature's web and are no more important than any other living creature. Therefore, the natural way is right, and human activities should be molded along nature's rhythms."

Also in the GBA: "Population growth has exceeded the capacity of the Earth, and to maintain our current global population of 5 to 7 billion people we must reduce our standard of living to that of an agricultural world in which most human beings are peasants. A reasonable population estimate for an industrialized society would be 1 billion people."

"To summarize other sections of the treaty, a heavy global tax would be levied on agriculture, forestry, mining and golfing. Heavy consumption taxes are to replace income taxes to discourage the use of automobiles, air conditioners and other items deemed non-essential to basic human needs." [11]

Part of the thrust of the Global Biodiversity Treaty is the creation of "Biospheres" and "World Heritage Sites," which have already placed many U.S. landmarks and national parks under the smiling stewardship of the U.N.. More than two-thirds of our U.S. national preserves, parks, and monuments, totaling about 51 million acres, have been tagged with these globalist designations, including Yosemite, Yellowstone, Glacier National Park, the Great Smoky Mountains National Park, the Everglades, Death Valley, Mammoth Cave, and Carlsbad Caverns — not to mention the Statue of Liberty and Independence Hall. [12]

Heralding the creation of these U.N.-controlled sites, Clinton signed Executive Order #12986, on January 18, 1996, which makes the administering body for the Biospheres and World Heritage Sites, a group called the International Union for Conservation of Nature and Natural Resources, immune from lawsuits, judicial process, and search and confiscation. This means that any activities whatsoever can be conducted by the U.N. controllers within the limits of Biosphere, and no-one can do anything about it. [13]

One of the "benefits" of global biodiversity which we will soon see is what is called "Border Region 21," based upon the La Paz Agreement, a portion of the sovereignty-busting, job-busting North American Free Trade Agreement (NAFTA). This agreement stipulates a "Border Environment Cooperation Project" will be created in a 60 mile-wide strip extending along the Mexican-American border through Arizona, California, New Mexico and Texas. This Border Region 21 will be jointly managed by the Americans and Mexicans — but why this strip of land is so important to internationalize, in distinction from many other areas in the U.S., is open to debate. It is interesting, however, that the land this project surrenders to joint Mexican-American management is precisely that which the Communist-linked Hispanic secessionist movement in the U.S. demands as tribute. [14]

What is going on is quite apparent to anyone venturing a small amount of study not limited to reading the *New York Times* or watching the NBC Nightly News. The political establishment in America, linked to globalist pirates worldwide, are hell bent on destroying the U.S. Constitution, and on creating a world-wide socialist state under the control of the U.N. Socialism for the poor 99% of the world's population, that is. Does anyone really believe that the Rockefellers, the Rothschilds, or any of their well-heeled compadres are going to hand over their jack in the interests of global biodiversity?

A one-world currency system will be instituted, along with a central world bank, and centralized economic, environmental and population control, along with regimentation of families along the lines of the U.N. Treaty on the Rights of the Child, wherein children are able to divorce their parents, and the government is able to move in and take control. Ask anyone who has recently participated in a child custody suit, or had dealings with social service workers — this is already happening. About all the social workers aren't doing, in their heavyhanded enforcement of the "rights of the child," is wearing black uniforms.

In this totalitarian New World Order so touted by men like Bush and Gorbachev, the U.S. military will be absorbed into the U.N., as per the stipulations of Publication 7277, and three world regional governments will be forged: The European Union, NACOM (Canada, Mexico, and the U.S.), and the Pacific Rim. These governments will iron out the kinks in member country's constitutions and traditions, silencing all dissenting voices and urging the transformation into a single "supranational" governing authority.

Worldwide, guns will be confiscated to quell any possible resistance to these measures, and new layers of social control legislation will be put in place — to continue to regiment our every move and our every thought into something closely resembling the Darth Vader regime we now observe in a place like Singapore. There you are monitored at every turn by cameras, controlled in thought, word and deed by legislation.

While media pundits, even rightwing ones like Rush Limbaugh, wave their arms vaguely, chuckle heartily, and deny that anything sinister is going on, even denying that there is any move toward a New World Order at all, the American populace by-and-large are aware that the American ideal has been devalued, the Constitution has been crushed, and that America is being ripped apart bodily by the forces creating world dictatorship.

NOTES:

1. Review of the United Nations Charter, Subcommittee on the United Nations Charter, 83rd Congress, January 1954
2. Jasper, William F., "A 'UN-Controlled World' Means Global Government. *The New American,* November 29, 1993
3. State Department Publication 7277, quotes taken from Relevance, 1994
4. Worldwide Peacekeeping Operations 1993, U.S. Central Intelligence Agency, government printing office
5. John F. McManus, "Steps Toward Tyranny," *The New American,* Volume 11, Number 7, April 3, 1995
6. Epstein, Edward, "Gorbachev Moves Into Presidio," *San Francisco Chronicle,* April 17, 1993
7. *Parade* magazine, January 23, 1994
8. "Beware the New World Army," *The New American,* April 20, 1992
9. Jasper, William F., "Global Green Regime," *The New American,* April 3, 1995
10. Kjos, Berit, "World Heritage 'Protection'," *Media Bypass* magazine, April 1997
11. "Diversity & Depopulation," *Nexus,* April/May 1997
12. Kramer, Bill, "U.N. Authority Imperils Freedom," *The Spotlight,* January 13, 1997
13. "U.N. Flexing Control Over Yellowstone," The *Patriot Report,* March 1996
14. Allen, Mike, "Border Area 21 — Calls for the Elimination of Border Between Mexico and U.S.," *The Independent,* reprinted in *The Free American,* April, 1997

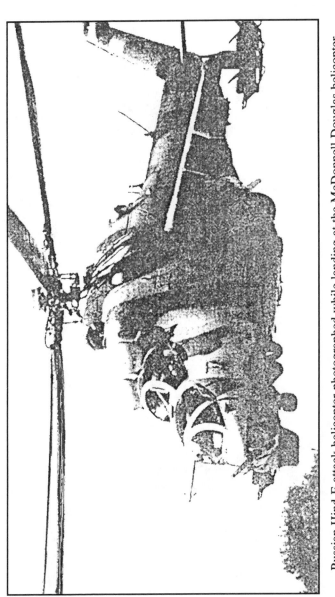

Russian Hind-E attack helicopter photographed while landing at the McDonnell Douglas helicopter production facility in Mesa, Arizona (Photo: *The Spotlight*).

1997 black helicopter photos by Robert A. Luca.

Black helicopter photo taken in Higganum, Connecticut in 1992
(Photo: Robert A. Luca).

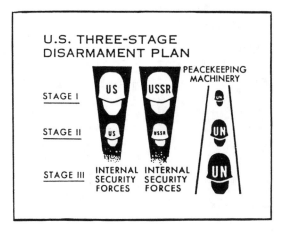

Source: "Second Annual Report to Congress," January 1, 1962 -
December 31, 1962. U.S. Arms Control & Disarmament Agency,
Publication 14, Page 11.

Aboard a train spotted in Montana were armored personnel carriers, some of which were painted white and bore the insignia of the United Nations (Photo: *The Spotlight*).

A number of what appear to be military satellite communications dishes have been placed at the Salt Lake City International Airport (Photo: *The Spotlight*).

A side view of one of the ZSU-23-4 radar-guided antiaircraft guns that were aboard a train photographed in Bay City, Michigan (Photo: *The Spotlight*).

Several rail cars carrying the Russian antiaircraft system that passed through Bay City, Michigan (Photo: *The Spotlight*).

Russian military vehicles in Ryegate, Montana (Photo: *The Spotlight*).

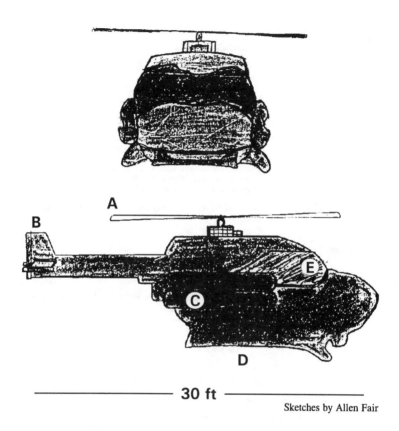

30 ft

Sketches by Allen Fair

A. Silent running rotor attached to finned aluminum type casing. Rotor small in relation to the body size of the helicopter.

B. Absence of a small rotor on tail. Short tail with rudder and vertical stabilizer, horizontal stabilizer (elevator?). Antennae extending from top of tail-fin.

C. Oddly shaped "tank" attachment. Design may be to assist in noise reduction.

D. Absence of landing gear. Underside concave, and lower in front than in rear.

E. Dark tinted windows.

DESTRON/IDI

Product Description:

The Injectable Transponder is a passive radio-frequency identification tag, designed to work in conjunction with a compatible radio-frequency ID reading system. The transponder consists of an electromagnetic coil, tuning capacitor, and microchip sealed in a cylindrical glass enclosure. The chip is pre-programmed with a unique ID code that cannot be altered; over 34 billion individual code numbers are available. When the transponder is activated by a low-frequency radio signal, it transmits the ID code to the reading system.

Although specifically designed for injecting in livestock, this transponder can be used for other animal and nonanimal applications.

Specifications:

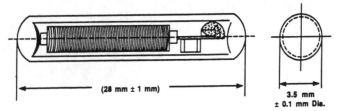

(28 mm ± 1 mm)

3.5 mm
± 0.1 mm Dia.

Dimensions (nominal): 28 mm by 3.5 mm (1.10" by 0.14")

Housing: Bio-compatible glass

Average weight: 0.77 g (0.027 ounces).

Temperature range: -40 to 70°C (-40 to 158°F), operating and storage

Read range with the Model HS5105L2 Mini-Portable Reader:
(In a benign noise environment with optimal orientation of transponder and scanner)

	Typical	Minimum
HS5105L2	33 cm (13")	30.5 cm (12")

Read speed: 3 meters per second

Vibration:
Sinusoidal; 1.5 mm (0.06") peak-to-peak, 10 to 80 Hz, 3 axis
Sinusoidal; 10 g peak-to-peak, 80 Hz to 2 kHz, 3 axis

Injector needle size: Approximately 7 gauge (Destron part # 445-0013-00/blunt tip and part # 445-0014-00/sharp tip).

Operating frequency: 125 kHz

Injectable Transponder
Suspiciously similar to those attributed to extra-terrestrials.

10

INVASION CHRONOLOGY

I n rapid-fire succession there have been more startling and historic New World Disorder turnabouts:

1994

— In January of 1994 there was a joint U.S./Russian "Arctic Rescue Training Exercises" at Fort Richardson, in Anchorage, Alaska. [1]

— $1.2 billion dollars was covertly diverted from the California Earthquake Relief Bill of February 13, 1994, for U.N.-sponsored U.S. military interventions in Bosnia, Somalia, and other regions. [2]

— On March 8, 1994 in Ryegate, Montana a 100-flatcar train was seen loaded with Russian military equipment, heading north. Witnesses report that it carried mostly BMP-40 Urban Pacification units, Kam AZ 5320 ZIL-31 trucks, and UAZ-469B jeeps. [3]

— On April 12, 1994 a convoy of armored vehicles of Russian make were seen on a highway 60 miles away from Dallas, Texas. [4]

— Between April 22, 1994 to May 11, 1994, 44,000 U.S., French, and Netherlands troops engaged in an exercise dubbed "Agile Provider 94" in the Southeastern U.S. Search and Seizure training was conducted in Gulfport, Mississippi, while home searches were conducted in this region by U.N. soldiers on April 25. [5]

— In April, 1994, U.S. fighter planes from NATO were ordered to Bosnia by British U.N. commander Sir Michael Rose and Japanese U.N. official Yasushi Akashi. Although President Clinton and Congress weren't informed (they wouldn't have given it a second thought, anyway), U.S. field commanders were quick to comply with standing orders to follow U.N. orders. [6]

— On May 3, 1994, President Clinton signed Presidential Decision Directive 25. This document includes provisions allowing U.S. soldiers to be transferred to United Nations command. [7]

— On May 10, 1994, at the Twenty-Nine Palms Marine Base in California, Marines were given a "Combat Arms Survey" that asked a number of disturbing questions, prompting a good deal of public furor when the contents of the survey got out. This questionnaire was also distributed among numerous other military units in the U.S. Among the questions posed:

"Do you feel that U.S. Combat troops should be used within the United States for any of the following missions?" The missions included "Drug enforcement," "Federal and state prison guards," "National emergency police force," and "Advisors to S.W.A.T. units, the FBI, or the Bureau of Alcohol, Tobacco, and Firearms (B.A.T.F.)."

Troops were asked to rate their agreement or disagreement with other statements, including, "It would make no difference to me to take orders from a U.N. company commander," "I feel the President of the United States has the authority to pass his responsibilities as Commander-in-Chief to the U.N. Secretary General," and "I would fire upon U.S. citizens who refuse or resist confiscation of firearms banned by the U.S. government."[8]

— According to an anonymous report, "On Tuesday May 31, 1994, at approximately 2:00 a.m., while traveling north on I-25, I witnessed three trains parked at what appeared to be a railroad junction just south of Wheatland, Wyoming. I also saw a fourth train moving east in the direction of the railroad junction. I was able to see part of the cargo on the three trains that were stopped. I identified the cargo as military equipment, consisting of tanks, APCs, two and a half ton trucks, and jeeps.

Some of the equipment was painted white, while others were dark in color. I also noticed men in dark uniforms running around the trains in what appeared to be 360 degree security. I am currently a military member who is highly trained in ground combat. At that time I was unable to positively identify the equipment and soldiers as being American or foreign. I was also unable to see the cargo on the fourth train. Two of the trains were pointing in a northerly direction, one was pointing south, and the moving train was headed east." [9]

— A Russian ship was seen unloading troops at a dockyard on Blount Island, Florida, on June 4th, 1994. Russian troops disembarked and boarded white buses (the U.N. painting scheme) with darkened windows, then proceeded south on Highway 95.

— The following report was received in June of 1994: "The Russian Red Banner Fleet is off the Gulf Coast, with four floating dry docks, with helicopters flying back and forth late at night. A light plane that went out to check on it was warned by radio when five-ten mile out to change course or be shot down." The fleet and the dry docks were docked at Gulfport, Mississippi on June 3, 1994.

The *Patriot Report* mentions that in "6-1-94, Soviet Black Sea Fleet ships practiced for an amphibious landing in the Gulf of Mexico. On this same date, four Russian Typhoon class submarines, equipped with ICBMs, docked at Mobile, Alabama, and five trains, each pulling over 100 flatcars, arrived at Fort Chaffee, Arkansas. Their cargo was over 1,500 pieces of U.N. equipment and large amounts of barbed wire.

Also in July, Russian helicopters were observed making nightly flights between the Russian ships and Gulfport, Mississippi. [10]

— "Reported & confirmed that there are now 19,000 German, Russian & Pakistani troops at Fort Polk, Louisiana; also foreign troops in Fort Carson, Colorado, and Fort Chaffee, Arkansas."

Also, "According to the military at Fort Chaffee, Arkansas, Agile Provider '94 ended its operation on June 26. Sources in the military said that German and Nigerian troops were on the base, to name only two foreign troops. The additional U.S. forces that took part in joint exercises at Fort Chaffee included the 82nd Airborne, and troops from Fort Sill, Oklahoma, Fort Benning, Georgia, and Fort Polk, Louisiana. What the operation called Agile Provider '94 was about has never been disclosed to the public. But one of the areas they trained the troops in was 'Forcible Entry.' Will that training be used against American citizens?"[11]

— On July 4, 1994, while in Russia, FBI Director Louis Freeh signed a protocol establishing increased cooperation between Russian and American law enforcement agencies. Freeh also agreed to open a Russian office of the FBI. [12]

— On July 4, 1994, 30 large military flatbed trucks were seen traveling on Interstate 25, near Denver, Colorado. Fifteen of the trucks were carrying wooden crates, while the other fifteen were transporting helicopters with U.N. lettering and call numbers on the sides. [13]

— The following letter, edited for length, was published by the *Patriot Report* in July, 1994:

> Topic: Russian/East Bloc T-72 tanks in West Texas. Date: June 12, 1994. Location: IH-10 westbound lanes, marker no. 258. Two semi trucks, two very large trailers, and a T-72 tank on each of these. Both truck tractors were solid white color [U.N. coloration] and on each door had a decal, rectangular in shape, 'Trism Specialty Carriers,' no address. Tanks: Definitely T-72 with full gear, the only item visibly absent was the 12.7 MM heavy machine gun, of course, stowed. Spare fuel drums were at the rear of the rear deck, and all else appeared combat ready. One T-72 appeared new or to have been completely refurbished and had a dark green/greenish gray camo scheme. The other T-72 had a more weathered look, light green/tan/dark green camo. A two digit number was seen on this one, whereas the number 'A30' was stenciled in white, relatively small, above the track and on the left front corner of the dark T-72. No unit or national markings were observed. [14]

— Joint operations of the San Francisco Police Department

and the elite Moscow Police Organized Crime-Fighting Regional Department took place in classrooms and on the streets of San Francisco in July, 1994. The Russians toured San Quentin prison, and attended seminars on high speed pursuit driving, narcotics enforcement, federal organized crime operations, surveillance, and hostage negotiation. [15]

— Two lieutenants stationed at Fort Benning, Georgia, refused to conduct 1,500 Russian troops on a tour of the base. The lieutenants were promptly taken into custody and removed to the stockade, then sent to Fort Bragg. [16]

— Received in July was a report from a retiring security policeman for the Air Force and National Guard, stating that Chinese Ghurkas from the British military had been conducting annual military training at the Yakima Training Center in Washington. He said that they had also done an amphibious assault in the area of Puget Sound, and that he had seen many British military trucks cruising I-90 and other areas of Washington, loaded with Ghurkas and other mercenaries. [17]

— On August 25, 1994 Russian SCUD-B surface-to-air missiles and an eight-wheeled MAZ-53 launch vehicle were observed being hauled on large flatbed trailers near Albuquerque, New Mexico, on Interstate 40. [18]

— According to the New York-based Russian newspaper *Novoye Russkoye Slovo,* "On Wednesday, a contingent of soldiers arrived at the military base near Tontsk (near Orenburg). They came to participate in conjunction with Russian soldiers in a military exercise under the name 'Worldcreator '94'... The communication agency 'Interfax' further reports that the Americans appeared along with a detachment of Police of Special Assignment (OMON) and rapid deployment soldiers from the Russian Ministry of Interior Affairs...

"The exercises will run from the second to the tenth of September. Nearly 250 soldiers from the United States and Russia will participate under the army generals Pavel Grachev and William Perry." [19]

— In the latter part of 1994 veterans groups issued written demands to President Clinton to withdraw his offer for the U.S.

to fund 2,500 Red Army officers with $25,000 housing vouchers each in their move from the Baltics to Russia, as well as building 5,000 housing units for the soldiers. Clinton replied in a letter to the veterans that the White House would continue to move ahead with the $160 million giveaway in an effort to ease strained relations between Russia and Latvia, Estonia, and Lithuania.

Bruce Theisen, national commander of the American Legion, replied by saying, "It's outrageous to see this policy enacted into law when nearly 17,000 American enlisted service men and women need foodstamps to subsist."

Richard W. Johnson, an official with the Non-Commissioned Officers Association, was also understandably bitter about the matter: "What you propose...is much more than what you have done for American GIs. He's buying out the Russian Army and selling out the U.S. Army." [20]

— In August of 1994, 21 German U.N. troops, all of the rank of colonel or above, set up a tent camp in rural Arizona near Wickenburg, about 40 miles northwest of Phoenix. A local sheriff's office spokesperson reported that the Germans were engaged in "desert survival exercises." Noting their presence, concerned locals visited the camp and told the U.N. group that they could either clear out or that they would be driven out by force. The Germans chose to decamp with dispatch.

Checking the Arizona license plates of the U.N. group, it was found that they were licensed to Lufthansa, the German national airline, headquartered at Goodyear Air Park, a former U.S. air base that has been turned over to Lufthansa. The air park is used for the training of German pilots. This is not the only U.S. airbase that has been deeded to the Germans. Holloman Air Force Base has also been turned into a German base, the first permanent foreign military base in America, with no Americans in the chain of command, and reporting to the German Air Force Command headquartered in Reston, Virginia. A portion of Fort Bliss has also been given to the Germans, with a landing strip and housing. [21]

— In September, 1994, Clinton sent tens of thousands of

U.S. troops into Haiti to enforce a U.N. resolution. Although a unanimous Senate resolution attempted to block Clinton's unconstitutional action, Clinton drawled a vague pretext of a "threat to international peace," and went ahead with the massive deployment. [22]

— "Since November, some 22,000 U.N. troops have arrived at Fort Bragg, including 10,000 Russian Spetsnaz and 5,000 Russian paratroops. The Russian troops are armed with AK rifles that shoot our 5.56 x 45 mm (.223) caliber ammunition and accept M-16 rifle magazines. Their Dragunov sniper rifles, as well as their squad machine guns are chambered for our 7.62 x 51mm NATO (.308) ammunition. This contact estimates that over 75,000 U.N. troops have been trained at Fort Bragg in the last few years." [23]

— Several hundred Russian and East German vehicles were seen at the Airmar Resources truck depot, south of Saucier, Mississippi in September, 1994. Many of these vehicles were reliably identified as Soviet nuclear, biological, and chemical warfare decontamination vehicles, but Air Force Lt. Col. Alfred Randolph Koval, Sr., when asked on the Radio Free America radio show, offered the cover story that they were "water trucks." [24]

— The New York-based Russian newspaper *Novoye Russkoye Slovo* reports that American soldiers are in Russia training to handle "cultural civil unrest." The newspaper reports that, "At this time, 'Blue Helmets' represent cooperative forces of special position. By statements from the American side, this represents having a big experimental work with a populated place. The exercises will be those of playing out the situation of 'cultural civil unrest.'" [25]

— On October 19, 1994, the International Association of Police Chiefs met in Albuquerque, New Mexico. In attendance were 7,000 police chiefs from all over the world. Internal documentation of the meeting defined American militia groups as terrorist organizations. [26]

— As reported in the December 21, 1994 *Orlando Sentinel,* titled "Army mum on what cargo U.S. brought from Russia,"

"A giant Russian cargo plane has delivered secret cargo to the Redstone Arsenal, a U.S. Army base in Huntsville, Alabama. Army officials admitted Tuesday that truckloads of material were delivered Monday to Alabama by a Russian An-124 aircraft. They would not say what the aircraft was carrying, only that it was not nuclear material and it did not pose a hazard. Because of its size, the An-124 had to use the Huntsville International Airport rather than the runway at Redstone." [27]

— As noted in the Alamogordo, New Mexico *Daily News* of December 25, 500 operational Russian tanks are in being stored at a "tank farm" at the White Sands Missile Range. According to the newspaper, other "tank farms are located at Eglin Air Force Base, Florida, Yuma Proving Ground, Arizona and Aberdeen Proving Ground, Maryland." [28]

— In December, 1994, approximately 1/2 block of crates of Pazgat black helmets, and a "warehouse full" of HK/MP5 machine guns were noted by LAPD workers as being in storage at the Los Angeles Police Department warehouse. [29]

— On December 1, 1994, the American sovereignty-busting General Agreement on Tariffs and Trade (GATT) and its World Trade Organization were approved by the Senate. A poll of the American public by the firm of Fabrizio and McLaughlin a week before the vote showed that seven out of ten citizens were against the WTO, but this did not dissuade our elected "representatives." [30]

— On December 16, 1994, Bill Clinton once again side-stepped the Constitution, and issued orders to send thousands of U.S. Marines to Somalia to bail out U.N. troops and to remove U.S. military equipment. [31]

— Also from the New York-based Russian newspaper *Novoye Russkoye Slovo,* "Nakhodka (on the seashore border). Five members of the Public Security Police Force had the honor of citizens in the American city of Bellingham [Washington]. The leader of the police, Bilal Rzayev, reported that not long ago, on a visit in the sister-city, they patrolled the streets together with American policemen, participating in the detention of law-breakers." [32]

— In 1994 the U.S. Army Reserve was reorganized to conform to the 10 national control regions stipulated by FEMA.[33]

1995

— Between January 26 and January 28, 1995, skiers observed approximately 120 U.S. Special Forces troops and Russian Spetsnaz involved in training exercises at the Bridger Ski Bowl area near Helena, Montana. [34]

— In February, 1995, a reserve crew member aboard a U.N. B-747 assigned to FEMA was traveling to the Federal Transfer Center in Oklahoma. Leaving the flight deck, he checked on the "prisoner cargo" and saw, aside from the usual black uniformed guards, " U.S. military officers, in Class A uniforms... gagged, cuffed, and shackled to their seats." [35]

— On February 28, 1995 a "pre-solicitation notice" was sent to contractors in New Mexico, notifying them that $10,000,000 to $25,000,000 would be spent to build a maintenance facility, office buildings, and landing area for the German Air Force. [36]

— At least nine Russian police officers visited several counties in South Carolina in March, 1995, in order to exchange information with their American counterparts. [37]

— In the early part of 1995, the Pro-Life Committee of Mexico and other groups protested that a U.N. program designed to provide a tetanus vaccine for women in Mexico is in fact a covert method of inducing abortions. Claims were based on analysis of the tetanus serum, which showed that it contained a tetanus toxoid as well as a human hormone dubbed hCG. The hCG hormone is used in developing anti-bodies which attack and terminate pregnancies. [38]

— In June, 1995, the first 34 police officers from the Czech Republic, Hungary, and Poland graduated from the FBI's International Law Enforcement Academy. Reaching out to the Eastern Bloc cops, Senator Orrin Hatch blubbered, "This is a major step forward in cementing U.S.-Hungarian relations. Help us save the West that has embraced you." [39]

— A published report in July 1995 spoke of the current state of the U.S. military: "My neighbor in the Naval Reserve was visiting this evening and mentioned that on his last (recent) two week stint in Seattle, a female in the Navy in Washington said that the young naval recruits were now being told that they had the 'choice' to 'voluntarily' exchange their uniforms for U.N. uniforms. When asked what would happen if they did not wish to don the U.N. uniform, she said, 'Well, they would be OUT.' That's voluntary?" [40]

— In August 1995, 600 Eastern Bloc troops were flown into Fort Riley, Kansas, for Peacekeeper '95, a joint training program with the Russians. This was supposedly done in a program exchange for American troops who were sent to Odessa in Russia in 1994.

The same month at Fort Polk, Louisiana, a military press release trumpeted, "Parachutes opened, marching music blared, and more than 4,000 members of three NATO and Central and Eastern Europe military services paraded across Honor Field here today to open Exercise Cooperative Nugget 95, the first NATO Partnership for Peace (PFP) exercise to be conducted in the United States."

U.S. Marine Corps Gen. John J. Sheehan remarked, "It is through services such as this that truly we can create a New World Order in which the militaries of the world can work in coordination and cooperation to build a better peace."

Included in press releases from the military was information on what the exercises entailed. Troops were taught to search buildings, vehicles and persons, and to create and supervise traffic checkpoints. They were given instruction in small arms and explosives, as well as what to do when encountering hostile civilians and those refusing to distribute food. Some of this training was done in mock American towns. Welcome to the New World Order.

— August 1995 was a big month for the cross training of international troops. The Santa Fe Railway magazine noted that their railroad had carried foreign war materiel from Beaumont, Texas to west and southern Texas for "Operation Roving

Sands," conducted by the military. Four trains and more than 400 rail cars were needed to transport Belgian and German military equipment, and more than 2,000 foreign troops were employed in the exercise. Roving Sands also featured joint training exercises utilizing 125 fighter aircraft and choppers, taking part in more than 1,500 sorties during the program. All of the equipment was shipped back to the port of Beaumont, Texas after the exercise. [41]

— While Russian and other Eastern Bloc soldiers were training in the U.S., American troops were training in Russia. The Associated Press reported, "Joint military exercises between Ukrainian troops and U.S. Marines are under way in the southern Ukrainian city of Odessa, Ukrainian military officials said Tuesday. 'The American Marines have landed, and everything is going smoothly,' Defense Ministry spokesman Ihor Melnichuk said. More than 300 Ukrainian soldiers and 800 Marines are taking part in 'Naval Marine Peace-making Mission-95.' The exercises mark a growing military relationship between the United States and the Ukraine." [42]

— A report from Montana: "On the morning of 9/13/95, my son and I were traveling west on I-90 at the Montana/Idaho border. A white semi truck was parked at the top of the pass alongside I-90. The truck was loaded with three white Humvees that were painted shiny white with black U.N. letters... We came back 9/14/95 in the evening and it was gone." [43]

— In September of 1995, the following anonymous letter appeared in a patriot newsletter:

"Earlier this decade, the U.S. Department of Transportation quietly adopted the U.N. regulations for the shipment of packaged (contained) commodities. This essentially gives control of material shipments within the U.S. to the U.N. Domestic as well as international shipments are controlled. The first phase of U.N. control started in 10/94 when U.N. containers were mandated for all nonbulk packaging instead of DOT containers. After 10/96, all vessels must meet U.N. standards. Fines of up to $500,000 and prison sentences of up to 5 years may be imposed for non-compliance. If one wishes to ship a container of household epoxy, he must comply with U.N. regulations. If anyone doubts that the shipment of goods is now controlled by the U.N., please look at the label attached to UPS packages containing nearly any hazardous chemical. You will find the U.N. code for that commodity with the letters U.N. followed by several numbers. It is hard for me to believe that our Congress and executive branch will allow the U.N. to control the American people. It appears, however, that that is exactly what they intend to do." [44]

— Touted as the first Russian military exercises in the U.S. (they weren't), in October of 1995 Fort Riley, Kansas played host to Russia's 27 Guards division. Although the specific size of the Russian force was not mentioned in press releases, the Associated Press said that, "The Russians will eat and sleep the soldier's life with American GIs here. Over the next 10 days they will learn how to handle new U.S. weapons technology, share ideas on such basic matters as guard duty and checkpoints, and talk strategy over how both sides might someday come together in a real joint peacekeeping endeavor." [45]

— On November 5 on a nationally televised call-in show, Thomas Pickering, the U.S. ambassador to Russia, admitted, "Yes, foreign troops are being based here, from Russia and from some other countries." Pickering said that the reason for bringing the "multinational" troops into the U.S. was to "familiarize them here and integrate and train them in peacekeeping operations and other operations like that." Pickering, in a fit of pique at being questioned said, "Next year there will be brigade-sized units coming from Russia, and maybe other U.N. nations, to familiarize them here." [46]

— Following a Freedom of Information Act request of the Pentagon by *Relevance* magazine, a chart was released showing the location of 145 foreign military vehicles in the U.S., supposedly all of the equipment that the Pentagon possesses. The chart was an obvious cover-up, and did not include, among other items, Russian choppers and SCUD and Frog missiles that have been observed and photographed in the U.S.

— 300 Russian troops in full battle gear arrived via a

Russian transport plane at Birmingham Airport in Alabama in December, 1995. [47]

— *The Rocky Mountain News* reported that "President Clinton has turned over about a ton of plutonium at Rocky Flats [nuclear facility in Colorado] to the United Nations as part of a historic effort to reduce the number of nuclear weapons world-wide." The U.N. was also given 199 tons of nuclear material at Department of Energy sites located in Oak Ridge, Tennessee, and Hanford, Washington. This amount comprises about one fifth of America's total stockpile of weapons grade material. The transfer of nuclear materials was supervised by a team from the International Atomic Energy Agency, based in Vienna. The team was headed by a Russian and included members from China and Vietnam. [48]

— Pennsylvania Air National Guardsman Sergeant Michael Smith, of the 193rd Special Operations Group, is another military man who has drawn a line in the sand over the New World Order. Sergeant Smith noted on his re-enlistment form that the document would not be binding be if the U.S. Constitution was suspended, or if he was told to 'exercise police powers' against Americans in a manner contrary to the Constitution. The National Guard didn't buy it, and lawyers for the Guard said that his stipulations suggested that his loyalty was to the people, as opposed "to the people, as expressed through their governmental institutions."

Smith said, "I just wanted to be sure that, if a situation ever developed where the Constitution I'd sworn to defend was tossed aside and I — as a member of a standing army — was ordered to act to the detriment of my fellow Americans, then I would have the legal right to terminate the enlistment."

To no one's surprise, Smith was refused re-enlistment. [49]

— At the end of 1995 Border Patrol and Army exercises began in the American/Mexican border states in preparation for "immigrant invasion," so said official participants. Events in Mexico such as the end of the cease-fire of the rebels in Chiapas state, and a deteriorating economy created speculation about increased waves of illegal immigration and perhaps even armed invasion.

Clinton administration Commissioner of the Immigration and Naturalization Service, Doris Meissner, tried to put the best face on the operations, saying that their purpose was not to send "threatening messages," to Mexico, but that, "We must handle emergencies if they arrive."

Assistant Chief Border Patrol Agent Dutch Steenbakker said, "We could call in other resources, the sheriff's department or the National Guard." Contradicting the statements of other officials, Steenbakker disclaimed that the exercise was specifically aimed at preparation for a Mexican border invasion, saying that there were "no particular scenarios... It could be a natural disaster, or the economy collapses, or the military attacks the government, or any number of other situations."

At the border in Nogales, Arizona, a "temporary collection point" was set up for dealing with illegals, consisting of a tent camp surrounded by barbed wire and supervised by armed guards. During an emergency, officials reported, the illegals would initially be gathered in Nogales and then dispatched to an "emergency detention center" near Tucson, Arizona. Depending upon the volume of illegals detained, "soft cover detention" facilities (i.e. tent cities) would be constructed. Noted was that buses from nearby cities would be commandeered for use in transporting illegals, if deemed necessary.

Although this news story was apparently featured only once in one newspaper in the U.S. media, illegal immigration comprises one of the greatest threats to the U.S. at this time.

"If [the current] level of immigration is not stopped, the U.S. population will soar from 250 million to 500 million over the next 50 years. To tolerate the way things are is to commit national suicide." So says Susu Levy, president of the Foundation for Optimal Planetary Survival, in Encino, California. Levy is correct. Although she terms it "national suicide," it would be more correct to refer to it as murder. The politicians and their owners know perfectly well what they are doing by allowing this massive influx of populace.

1996

— On January 23, 1996, Army Specialist Michael New (not to be confused with Sergeant Michael Smith, above) was convicted of disobeying a "lawful order" due to his refusal to wear a U.N. uniform. He was subsequently discharged from the U.S. Army. This ruling was in complete contradiction to U.S. Army regulations concerning "Wearing and Appearance of Army Uniforms and Insignia," specifically paragraph 1-4a of AR 670 where it is specifically noted that "only uniform, accessories, and insignia prescribed in this regulation or in the Common Table of Allowances (CTA), or as approved by Headquarters, Department of the Army (HQDA) will be worn by personnel in the U.S. Army."

According to New, "I'm proud to wear the U.S. Army uniform for what it represents. A lot of good men have bled in the same uniform for my country and I am not willing to take it off to fight for a foreign government."

Daniel New, Michael's father, offered the following comments: "This country is involved in a constitutional crisis. Our very national sovereignty is at stake. Any time the army of a nation can be forced to serve a foreign power, then that country is not a sovereign power. This republic stands on the brink of being delivered into a one-world government by a president who took an oath to support and defend the same Constitution that Specialist Michael New did."

Daniel New also jabbed at the complacency of Americans: "No man who stands on truth can really lose. But we need to know if the republic has died. Perhaps America will observe a moment of silence at half-time of the Super Bowl in memory. If we lose because the rules have been changed, then what has happened is the republic has died, and they forgot to print the whole story. And if this whole thing with my son brings that into focus then it will have served its purpose." [50]

— At the beginning of 1996, U.N. Secretary-General Boutros Boutros-Ghali publicly called for the direct taxing of the people of the world by the United Nations. Boutros-Ghali suggested that the tax might be a surcharge on airline tickets, or a fee charged for the exchange of foreign currencies. Boutros-Ghali came close to turning on the tears when he said, "We would not be under the daily financial will of member states who are unwilling to pay up."

As outrageous as the idea of a U.N. tax or taxes is, the American public apparently goes along with the idea. A survey by the Americans Talk Issues Foundation produced the following answers:

72% of the surveyed public felt that U.N. resolutions should "rule over the actions and laws of individual countries... even the laws of the United States."

86% responded favorably when the idea of the U.N. arresting a president of the United States convicted of wrongdoing was proposed.

76% of the surveyed wanted the U.N. to become "policeman to the world."

The survey also said, "overwhelming majorities of Americans" support the U.N. taxing the world in just about any context. [51]

— "On the morning of Tuesday, 3/19/96, a large flatbed commercial carrier was photographed as it passed through Yellville, Arkansas. The truck was traveling on AR 62 at the time. The cargo was three U.N. equipment items. At the forward station was a small trailer mounted generator set. Center was a Humvee rigged as an ambulance without any Red Cross markings. Aft was a Humbee with no right door visible in the photo. All equipment is painted white with black U.N. insignia. [52]

— As of May 1996, a division of NASA moved into a facility located at Moses Lake, Washington termed "the Base" by locals. The location has what is reported to be one of the longest airport runways in the world, and ten to fifteen jets with Japanese Airlines markings were landing there every day at this time. Also, black, unmarked cargo planes were flying in three at a time, unloading, and then taking off, with trains coming into the Base, but only at night. Reports state that security on this base is tight. [53]

— *The Gazette Telegraph* provided the following report: "The United States and Russia will test missile-defense procedures in a joint computer exercise in June at Falcon Air Force Base east of Colorado Springs, a senior defense official said Thursday... The tests will involve the use of simulators against third-party attackers, said Ashton Carter, Assistant Secretary of Defense for International Security Policy. No missiles will be fired. Speaking to defense reporters at a breakfast meeting, Carter said the exercise June 3-7 will take place under the auspices of the U.S. Space Command and be at the Joint National Test Facility at Falcon AFB." [54]

— Reports have been received that many high ranking military officers have resigned from the military, including three-star generals. According to one source, "It seems that 56 days ago all military officers were told that they must agree with the coming military agenda. Anyone who did not want to go along would be given an honorable discharge. Anyone who did not make a decision within this 100 days would be given a dishonorable discharge. In addition, General Shalikashvili (Chairman of the Joint Chiefs of Staff) was ordered to change the UCMJ (Uniform Code of Military Justice) so that any soldier or officer not obeying any order, regardless of whether or not such order is lawful or constitutional, will be court marshaled." [55]

The above information was verified by *Perceptions* magazine, which mentioned the report of "a Marine non-commissioned officer who deals with colonels and above." According to this man, "The joint chiefs have rewritten the Uniform Code of Military Justice to state that the United States will accept orders and command from the United Nations." [56]

— On July 4, 1996, a gathering of California citizens protesting illegal aliens in Westwood, California were attacked by a group of red-shirted persons armed with clubs, allegedly organized by a coalition including the Communist Progressive Labor Party [PLP], the Asian Pacific Islanders for Immigrant's Rights and Empowerment [API FIRE], the UCLA Asian-Pacific Coalition, Central American Resource Center [CARACEN], the Coalition for Humane Immigrant Rights of Los Angeles [CHIRLA], the Committee in Solidarity with the People of El Salvador [CISPES], and the L.A. Gay/Lesbian Service Center. Many of the protesters were injured, and when the LAPD Riot Squad arrived, 15-20 minutes after the violence had started, they are reported to have observed attacks on unarmed protesters without making arrests. [57]

— Marine Corps personnel from Camp Lejeune, North Carolina conducted urban warfare exercises in the Mobile and New Orleans areas between August 19-29. The training involved helicopter flights and urban training, using live fire. It was also reported that Russian troops were involved in the training, including Russian support ships based in the Gulf of Mexico. [58]

— Late in 1996, 200 Canadian Armed Forces Rangers joined several hundred troops from Eastern Bloc countries at Fort Shelby, Mississippi, to take part in operation "Roguish Gator." Troops from the operation entered DeSoto National Forest and stopped civilians from entering on roads leading into the forest.

Other curious activities have been noted in the DeSoto National Forest. Quoting *The Spotlight* newspaper, "Mississippi civilians have discovered a secret military base, manned by civilian and U.S. and foreign military personnel, deep within the DeSoto national Forest in the southeastern part of the state.

"The base, located within a restricted area of the national forest, posted with signs designating it as an 'endangered species' habitat, covers a considerable area. Abundant about the base were Russian T-72 main battle tanks, TBR-60 Russian armored personnel carriers, a SCUD surface-to-surface missile battery consisting of several individual units and missiles, at least one Russian SA-6 Gainful surface-to-air (SAM) missile launcher with its three missiles elevated and in launch position and a Russian SA-8 Gecko SAM carrier with its four missiles in place."

Similar activity has been taking place in Louisiana, at the Kisatchie National Forest located adjacent to the Fort Polk military base. Fort Polk has been the center for the training of thousands of foreign troops. The Pentagon has proposed the annexing of 85,000 acres of the national forest for the expansion of Fort Polk, and for a bombing range for the Air Force. The Louisiana National Guard has also requested more than 10,000 acres of the national forest for a training base. [59]

— *Wake Up Call America,* a small newspaper published in Colorado, provides this update: "There are reports of large numbers of foreign troops and equipment throughout the U.S., Canada, and Mexico. One of the most credible accounts comes from Jim Ammerman, a WWII Air Force vet who became a head chaplain afterwards... About 18 months ago Jim estimated that there were about 30,000 foreign troops in America. Six months ago he upped that to 80,000 troops. Recently he has had contact with two U.S. congressmen and one U.S. senator who are quite concerned about the situation and confided to Jim that the number he was using was way off. When Jim asked them what the number was, they said in all three countries it is now over 3,000,000 — yes, that is not a misprint, he was told three million foreign troops are positioned throughout North America today. Jim gave one account of a Mexican national who had just traveled the length of Mexico south to north who said that the Russian troops were so thick that they were buying up all the food in some areas and creating a shortage for the Mexican people..." [60]

1997

— May, 1997: "I hold patriot group meetings in my home in Boulder, Colorado, and I have some bits to pass on to you. On two separate occasions large convoys have been sighted heading west, out of town. They consist of white personnel transports and trucks, carrying artillery and tanks. The trucks are unmarked except for numbers painted on the doors and hood. Both eyewitness accounts have placed the drivers of these vehicles as being dressed in white with no patches or insignia. We have also spotted formations of between 4 and 10 black helicopters on several occasions outside of town." [61]

— An Associated Press news release for April 8, 1997:

> Brisbane, Australia (AP) — The U.S. Marine Corps said today it is investigating how its military police behaved last month while arresting several Aborigines outside a nightclub. A civil rights group and advocates for Aborigines say Queensland police and U.S. military police used excessive force in making the arrests, including punching and kicking Aborigines. The scuffle in Ipswich, captured on security video cameras, occurred two weeks ago when U.S. military personnel were stationed at Amberley air base, west of Brisbane, for combined military exercises called Tandem Thrust.

What were U.S. Marines doing making arrests with Australian police in a Tandem Thrust? [62]

— Sources in Canada are concerned, noting that the country has "opened her doors wide to NWO military forces, including German, Russian, and Chinese." Also mentioned is that next to Dease Lake, in Canada, Germans have been deeded a military air base for their use, and are actively practicing military maneuvers including bombing and strafing by aircraft. Russians and Chinese have had an increasing presence in Canada, and have been involved in the renovation and strengthening of railroad tracks throughout the country. [63]

NOTES:

1. "Police State Activities in America," *Patriot Report* Info Packet, September 1995
2. McManus, John F., "Steps Toward Tyranny," *The New American,* Volume 11, Number 7, April 3, 1995
3. "Police State Activities in America"
4. "More Russian Tanks in America," *Patriot Report,* July 1994
5. "Police State Activities in America"
6. McManus
7. "Police State Activities in America"
8. Intelligence Briefing, December 1994; "New World Order Combat Arms Survey," *The Resister,* Volume 1, Number 2. Autumn 1994
9. Anonymous report
10. Freedom's Ring, August/September 1994; "More Russian Tanks in America," *Patriot Report,* July 1994, September 1995 Info Packet

11. "News Briefs and National Rumors," *Patriot Report*, July 1994
12. Intelligence Briefing; McAlvany, Donald, "Beware of the Bear: The Russian Strategy for World Domination. *The McAlvany Intelligence Advisor*, March 1995
13. "Police State Activities in America"
14. "More Russian Tanks in America"
15. Wallace, Bill, "S.F. Cops Teach Russians to Fight Crime," *San Francisco Chronicle*, July 25, 1994
16. "More Russian Tanks in America"
17. "Letters to the Editor," *Patriot Report*, July 1994
18. "Police State Activities in America"
19. "Worldcreator 94," Soldiers '94
20. "Clinton Houses Red Army," The *Washington Times*, September 1, 1994
21. Blair, Mike, "Armed Patriots Confront U.N. Unit," *The Spotlight*, September 12, 1994; Ammerman, Colonel Jim. "Imminent Military Takeover of the U.S.A., spoken presentation to the Prophecy Club
22. McManus
23. "National News Briefs," *Patriot Report*, April 1995
24. *The Spotlight*, October 3, 1994
25. *Novoye Russkoye Slovo*, September 6, 1994, translated by J. Braxton James
26. "Police State Activities in America"
27. "Army mum on what cargo U.S. brought from Russia," *Orlando Sentinal*, December 21, 1994
28. "Working on the Tank Farm," Alamogordo, New Mexico *Daily News*, December 25, 1994
29. "Updates from Southern California," Silver State II newsletter, February 19, 1995
30. *The Spotlight*, December 19, 1994
31. McManus
32. *Novoye Russkoye Slovo*, December 20, 1994, translated by J. Braxton James
33. "Police State Activities"
34. "Police State Activities"
35. *Seventieth Week* magazine, reprinted in the *Patriot Report*, June 1995 information packet
36. "U.S. Taxpayers to Build a New German Air Force Aircraft Maintenance Facility in New Mexico," *Taking Aim* newsletter, March, 1995

37. The *Lincoln Gazette,* March 12, 1995
38. "U.N. Accused of Tampering with Tetanus Vaccine for Third World," *Patriot Report,* October 1995
39. *Arkansas Democrat Gazette,* June 17, 1995
40. "National News Briefs," *Patriot Report,* July 1995
41. "U.S. & Foreign Soldiers Train in Louisiana," *Patriot Report,* September 1995; "2000 Foreign Troops train in Texas, New Mexico," The *Patriot Report,* August 1995
42. "800 U.S. Marines land in Ukraine," Associated Press, quoted in the *Patriot Report,* September, 1995
43. "National News Briefs," *Patriot Report,* December, 1995; Blair, Mike, "Russian Troop Sightings Replaced Eastern Bloc Vehicles as Populist Reconnaissance Increased," *The Spotlight,* December 1, 1996
44. The *Patriot Report,* September 1995
45. "Russians hold first exercises in U.S.," Associated Press, October 27, 1995
46. Mann, Martin, "Foreign Forces to Increase Here," *The Spotlight,* November 21, 1994
47. Blair, Mike, "Russian Troop Sightings Replaced Eastern Bloc Vehicles as Populist Reconnaissance Increased," *The Spotlight,* December 1, 1996
48. Rocky Mountain News, December 17, 1995; "Clinton turns over U.S. plutonium to United Nations," *New American,* January 22, 1996
49. "Allegiance Not Acceptable," We Hold These Truths, January 1996; Blair, Mike, "Guardsman Ousted After Refusing to Serve 'New World Order' Against U.S." *The Spotlight,* December 25, 1995
50. "Soldier Ousted Over Insignia," Associated Press, undated clipping; "Army S.P.C. New Found Guilty, Given Discharge," *Patriot Report,* March 1996
51. Tucker, Jr., James P., "U.N. Head Flies Tax Trial Balloon," *The Spotlight,* January 29, 1996; Tucker, James P. "Poll: Americans Surrender Sovereignty," *The Spotlight,* September 11, 1995
52. News release from Militia of Washington County, Arkansas, March 1996
53. "National News Briefs," *Patriot Report,* May 1996
54. "Russians Coming to Falcon," *Gazette Telegraph* and news service, May, 1996
55. Fax received from H & M, June 1996

56. "Military Officers Told to Obey NWO Agenda or Quit," *Patriot Report,* June 1996
57. "U.S. Citizens Attacked by Communists," *Patriot Report,* September 1996
58. "Late Breaking News," *Patriot Report,* October 1996
59. Blair, Mike, "U.S. Wants Your Land," *The Spotlight,* December 16, 1996; The Spotlight, September 30, 1996
60. "Russian Troops Buying Food Create Shortages for Some Mexicans," Wake Up Call America
61. Anonymous, correspondence with the author, May 8, 1997
62. Associated Press, April 8, 1997
63. "Massive Build-Up of Foreign Troops in Canada & Mexico," *Patriot Report,* December 1996

11

INSIDE THE CAMPS

After Russia, America could be called the most imprisoned country on earth. In 1994 inmates of American prisons topped one million in number — and this does not include the number of persons in jails. Twenty-six percent of the persons incarcerated are illegal aliens. If one million prisoners sounds like a lot, consider the prediction voiced during an HBO special on January 1, 1996. That presentation projects that by the year 2015 the prison population of America will be six million inmates. [1]

Although there are certainly no shortage of prisons in this country, for several years there has been concern about the proliferation of secret sites in the United States, apparently constructed for use as detainment centers (read concentration camps). Since the 1970s there has been created a secret and vast infrastructure of facilities for imprisonment that has caused much speculation about their intended purpose. At least 43 of these sites are acknowledged by the government, but many others have been reported to exist.

Fueling speculation is an August 29th, 1994 Department of the Army memorandum titled "Draft Army Regulation on Civilian Inmate Labor Program." The first paragraph defines the purpose of the memo, stating, "Enclosed for your review and comment is the draft Army regulation on civilian inmate labor utilization and establishing prison camps on Army installations."

Here is an update on some of these facilities. For information on additional sites see the first book in this series.

— Fort Huachua, Arizona: Located near the Mexican border, in a rural area of Arizona, this is one of the original FEMA Rex 84 camps. U.N. soldiers have allegedly been sighted in this location. [2]

— Fort Chaffee, Arkansas: This location contains a detention center capable of holding 25,000 persons. It is one of the key facilities activated during the Reagan administration in the FEMA Rex 84 plan. Much construction work has recently been done at the camp, along with massive amounts of barbed wire shipped in, and a reported 5,000 mattresses. A new airplane runway has also reportedly been built. This camp has been used in recent years for the training of foreign soldiers. [3]

— Oakdale, California: This is another of the camps built during the FEMA Rex 84 contingency program. This camp is located 90 miles east of San Francisco, on Highway 120, and is reportedly large enough to hold 15,000 prisoners. [4]

— Vandenberg Air Force Base: This base, located between San Luis Obispo and Santa Barbara, on the California coast, was activated as a detention facility during Rex 84. The base is located next to Highway 1. [5]

— Avon Park, Florida: This detention center was built during World War II, and is listed in official publications as Avon Park Correctional Institute. The facility is officially closed, but that designation has not slowed down the large amount of activity that is taking place there. Foreign military equipment and white U.N. vehicles have been seen in this location.

— Elgin Air Force Base: This is another large facility activated during the Rex 84 program. It covers more than 50 miles of territory. [6]

— Panama City, Florida: Built east of Panama City, in Calhoun County, in Florida, this facility is constructed as a psychiatric prison, with a similar one also built in Lubbock, Texas. The prison is surrounded in barbed wire, has gun towers, rail service, and an airstrip. [7]

— Abbeville, Georgia: "Wilcox Correctional Institute," is located in Wilcox County, south of Abbeville, on Highway 129. It is 20 acres by approximately 60 acres, with an estimated holding capacity of 20,000 prisoners. The facility is fully staffed at this time, but without prisoners. There is easy accessibility by highway and railroad. [8]

— Fort Benning, Georgia: This Army base is located near Columbus, Georgia, and is another of the original facilities built during the Reagan administration's Rex 84 plan. [9]

— Hawkinsville, Georgia: This detention facility is located in Pulaski County on Fire Road 100, two miles west from Alternate 129, 5 miles east of Hawkinsville. This is a woman's facility, built to very modern standards, with peach colored paint. Its estimated capacity is 15,000 prisoners. It is currently fully staffed, without prisoners. This facility is easily accessed by highway and railroad. [10]

— McCrae, Georgia: Located in Telfair County, 1-1/2 miles west of McRae on Highway 341, this facility is approximately 15 acres by 40 acres. It has an estimated capacity of 20,000 prisoners. Fully staffed at this time, there are no prisoners there currently, according to my information. There is easy accessibility by highway and railroad. [11]

— Morgan, Georgia: Located in Calhoun County, here is a facility of approximately 10 acres by 30 to 40 acres. Its estimated capacity is 15,000 prisoners. It is currently fully staffed, without prisoners. Again, easy accessibility by railroad and highway. [12]

— Oglethorpe, Georgia: This facility is located in Macon County, five miles from Montezuma. Traveling south on Highway 49, the detainment center is on the west side of the highway. It is approximately 10 acres by 30 acres, with an estimated capacity of 15,000 prisoners. There are currently no staff or prisoners at the site. [13]

— Unadilla, Georgia: In Dooley County, on E. Railroad Street, Plunkett Road leads into the facility. It is approximately 10 acres by 35 to 40 acres, with an estimated capacity of 15,000 prisoners. This detainment center is currently manned and staffed, without prisoners. It is accessed from highway and railroad. [14]

— Marseilles, Illinois: Here is a 300' by 300' location,

enclosed with barbed wire, with observation towers at four corners. Approximate capacity: 1,400 detainees.

— Indianapolis, Indiana: According to source formerly employed by the Joint Chiefs of Staff, "There is a death camp at Beech Grove, in the southeast quadrant of Indianapolis. There are ten maintenance barns at the Amtrak repair facility that have received so much attention from Linda Thompson and Mark Koernke that they have set up an open house tour of the place on the first Saturday of every month. You've got to know what you're looking for, if you get to go through the tour as I did. (An Amtrak guard told me that the guards there have even been issued black uniforms; he had his in his locker.) "

It is a 129-acre facility with fences on the outside with the tops leaning inward. The second fence on the inside also has the fence tops leaning in. The windows of the building have been bricked up. Hence you have three levels of security for an Amtrak repair barn!

"There are three 25-knot helicopter wind socks (which are not the correct ones to use for chemical spills; you use 10-knot wind socks for chemical spills). These buildings of this old 1910 facility have had $6 million dollars in repairs and upgrades. There are high security turnstiles, high security lighting, and signs which mark red and blue zones. One of the barns is large enough to put four boxcars into, and there are vents on the top.

"They're only going to handle category 1 and 2 (red and blue) people there; there will be no 'green' people handled. This facility will be used for execution and maximum security."

A later note from the same source reports, "The Beech Grove (Indianapolis, Indiana) 'four boxcar' gas chamber which I personally toured and took pictures of in 6 August of 1994, has been 'sanitized.' They took down the 'Red/Blue Zone' signs, and the NSA-type turnstiles." [15]

— Grayling, Michigan: The following report on detention facilities in the vicinity of Grayling, Michigan is provided by researcher Harold R. Green, Jr. A number of detention facilities have been built in this area, and Mr. Green speculates on their use.

Green also mentions the "Quadrant Sign Encoding System," a directional system employing reflective markers. This system has been noted around the nation, and is treated in more detail in the next chapter. The following information is printed with permission:

It has been interesting to observe the Department of Transportation in our area preparing the roadways with the Quadrant Sign Encoding System on the backs of Michigan road signs for what is obviously some kind of future military 'coup de main.' Even someone with limited knowledge of strategic warfare would find it hard to deny that facilities and markers targeted by these highly reflective markers are vital, and if confiscated, would give instant superiority to an invasionary force over a helpless populace.

Most interesting to take note of is the network of routes that lead to prisons, detention facilities, and center marked by M.DOT [Michigan Department of Transportation] with 'Facility Symbols.' During the road sign marking of these facilities, Camp Lehman, Camp Pugsley, and Shawono Center, have received 'Maximum Security' upgrades, while their official status still remains 'Minimum Security.' Guards and correctional officers have been given 'arrest powers' as newly erected compound perimeter signs declare felony charges to any trespassing person on 'Prison Property.' As you will notice, all of this has very little to do with the keeping and securing of the incarcerated, but has everything to do with keeping the public out! Is there something that the Department of Corrections does not want the public to know or see concerning these marked facilities?

The 'Shawono Center,' located about three miles west of Grayling, Michigan, is a good case in point. This detention facility, located also on the property of the Camp Grayling Military Reserve, has been marked on its highway facility signs with a large, reflective, blue 'TAC-MARK turn indicator' by the Special Crews arm of the Michigan Department of Transportation. Shawono is a rather small facility designed as a drug rehabilitation site for youth, but went through a rather elaborate facelift during the years 1992-93. A new detention wing was added, consisting of about 30 new cells (very small in dimensions), and a very sophisticated computer system in a glass-encased control room.

About this same time, the U.S. Army began doing helicopter

landings and other training maneuvers on this site and on a small man-made lake adjacent to Shawono. All hunting was banned from surrounding wooded areas also. In 1995-96 all small trails and two-track roads around Shawono were blocked off by large beams buried in the ground two feet apart and four feet high. Signs were also erected on these barriers stating: RESTORATION AREA, NO MOTORIZED VEHICLES ALLOWED" BY ORDER OF DEPT. OF MILITARY AFFAIRS. On the northwest and north perimeters of Shawono Center, small, reflective yellow signs on steel stakes were planted along the roadside, stating: KEEP OUT, THREAT-ENED AND ENDANGERED SPECIES. As of this writing, guard rails have been added to the road barriers.

This is all very strange activity for the Department of Military Affairs! Oddly, a 1-800 number was included on one of the barrier post signs, which I called the next day. A nice fellow from the Military Affairs Department answered and I inquired as to the added features at the Shawono Center. He began to explain how the four-wheelers and dirt bikes have been tearing up the area and that they were re-seeding the grassy areas to restore its natural beauty. When I asked, 'What threatened and endangered species are there?' there was a rather lengthy pause, after which he sheepishly uttered, 'Well, there aren't really any endangered species there, but the grass and flowers need to be protected from the abuse they are getting, so we put up the signs just to keep them out of there.' How sweet, that the Department of Military Affairs is so interested in the welfare and beauty of grass and flowers!

This also proves the military is behind many of the fraudulent signs being erected about endangered species, zoo annexes, and the like, to keep the public away from sensitive areas they are preparing for treasonous activities. While in the 'restoring mode' it is inter-esting that the military didn't fill in an abandoned gravel pit next to a grassy hill they seeded, just a few hundred yards from Shawono.

My opinion of the Shawono Center is yet uncertain; but it has the earmarks of a possible future extermination camp. Of all the prison camps in the area, it is the smallest. It is the only BLUE stickered facility by the D.O.T. It is the only detention facility where helicopter landings and military exercises have been ob-served in the area. It has a ready-made burial pit in close proximity. Shawono is on a route that is networked to two other prisons, and a newly discovered POW style sorting facility with seven guard towers on range 3 area, in the Camp Grayling Military Reserve. It is gradually being closed off to the public, and the military is behind it, and is lying about it." [16]

— Pearl River, Mississippi: This location has been used for the detainment of Haitian refugees, and for overflow prisoners from Hancock County.

— Winnemucca, Nevada: Located between Lovelock and Winnemucca, off I-80 at mile marker 112. Seen at this location are rows of barracks, surrounded with fences topped with razor wire. There are also reported to be an airfield and hangars. Russian planes and soldiers are also reported to have been seen at this location. This site has an estimated capacity of 5,000 prisoners. [17]

— Fort Dix, New Jersey: Confirmation of activity at Fort Dix, New Jersey is provided by a letter to the editor of the *Patriot Report,* from an inmate in Georgia:

"My job here in the institution is located in the Mattress Factory, Prison Industries (UNICOR). Recently we received an order for 1,800 bunk-style mattresses to be delivered on or before 12/24/96 to Fort Dix, New Jersey. The interesting part of the order is that the billing for the mattresses is not to the military, but to the Department of Justice!" [18]

— Fort Drum Military Reservation, New York: This is another of the key detention camps, capable of holding 25,000 persons, and activated by the Reagan administration during the FEMA Rex 84 plan. This location is close to the Canadian border, and much black helicopter activity is seen in this area, reportedly being flown from a U.N. base located in Canada. [19]

— Seneca Army Depot, New York: Located about 20 miles west of the Syracuse, New York is a military base that has been announced for closing, but instead is being turned into a federal detention center. This information is based upon the reports of locals who have received contracts for reconstruction of the facility, and the installation of chain link fence and barbed wire. There are many over-flys of black helicopters coming from Fort Drum, New York, and black choppers are also using the private Finger Lakes Regional Airport at Seneca Falls. There, white cars, trucks and vans with government license plates have been seen frequently entering and leaving the facility. [20]

— Camp Buckner, North Carolina: An anonymous military source reports, "There are two massive prisons at Camp Buckner, built side-by-side. One was built earlier, and the other was built only last year. The thing is about a half-mile square, is barb-wired, and has a helicopter control tower in the middle of it." [21]

— Oklahoma City, Oklahoma: Again, a military source requests anonymity with the following report. It is reprinted with permission:

> I've talked to a general officer who has been to Oklahoma City and seen the Federal Transfer facility there. I have pictures of it and have put the pieces together. They were forced in April, 1995 to declare the facility, and they held an open house on April 4. On April 7, they admitted that they had a prisoner airline with twelve 747s operating out of 38 cities, with 'feeder lines.' These feeder lines were the 3,000 black helicopters that Bush signed over to the Treaty on Open Skies. The feeder lines will feed the transfer facility from the intermediate sites...
>
> To control these helicopters they must have a control network where they can communicate without going through the FAA. I'm a pilot myself, and that's how I've figured this out. All around the country they have AWOS (Automatic Weather Observation System) towers, built by Scan Corporation. These are little towers alongside the road which have a spinner on top with a couple of little canisters hanging off; sometimes they have a fence around them. The towers have no markings on them. It gives you a terminal weather forecast; all the weather information that the helicopter pilot has to have to operate. To access the terminal weather forecast on that tower (which has a telephone number) he has a cellular telephone system. There is a telephone number on the cellular telephone system that they can use to call the tower in the area they will operate in. The pilot must know the weather forecast at the terminal area he is going in to. They call in on the cellular system and get the information they need; they do not have to call in with their copped accents to

the FAA Flight Service Station to get the weather forecast. Just last year they banned all scanners from the cellular phone frequencies.[22]

Bill Lord, a prisoner at the Federal transfer center in Oklahoma City, informs us that the facility is currently being run by Australians. [23]

— Tinker Air Force Base, Oklahoma: This is the site of another detention camp. The location also contains a mock American village where the Air Force and others train for SWAT-style tactics.

— Allenwood, Pennsylvania: linked to Interstate 80, this site covers approximately 400 acres, surrounded by a 10 foot barbed wire fence. During the 1970s it held 300 minimum security prisoners, but could potentially hold 12,000 persons.

— Camp Hill, Pennsylvania: This large facility, capable of holding a reported 25,000 prisoners, was activated during the Reagan administration in the FEMA Rex 84 plan, and is located off Interstate 15. Nearby are the New Cumberland Army Depot and the Camp Hill Correctional Facility. [24]

— Fort Indiantown Gap, Pennsylvania: This is another large detention center activated during the Reagan era under the Rex 84 plan. It was used to hold thousands of Cubans during the Mariel boat lift. This location has been the site of extensive training exercises involving the military and FEMA.

— Amarillo, Texas: This detention center is located near Lake Meredith, Interstate 40, U.S. 87, and Interstate 27. It is in proximity to trains and an airport. It is a possibly significant location because of reports of U.N. and multi-jurisdictional forces already stationed there. [25]

— Fort Hood, Texas: This military installation is alleged to have a new detainment center built within its confines, including barracks and watch towers. It is surrounded by fences and barbed wire. Base personnel are forbidden to enter this section.[26]

— Lubbock, Texas: Psychiatric detention facility replete with barbed wire fences and watch towers.

— Odessa, Texas: This is the location of the Eckert County

Detention Facility, with an estimated capacity of 140 prisoners. It is part of the "prisons for profit" program. Black uniformed guards are seen coming and going from this facility. [27]

— Seattle, Washington: Here is a modern prison and/or transfer center run by FEMA. The facility is located at the south end of the SeaTac airport, S. 200th St. and 26th Avenue S. [28]

— Fort McCoy, Wisconsin: This is one of the original Rex 84 facilities, located 30 miles northeast of Lacrosse, between Interstate 90 and 94. I received the following information from a civilian employee of the Department of the Army, and an active Army reservist. For obvious reasons, this person chooses to remain anonymous. His account is reprinted with permission:

Validation — You show Fort McCoy, Wisconsin as a possible concentration camp. It has in fact already been used for that very purpose. As you may recall, the summer of 1979 gave us waves of Cuban 'boat people' as Castro gave his fiefdom an enema with the nozzle pointed at American soil. I was an Army Reservist on Annual Training (AT) at Ft. McCoy at that time. An engineer unit at Ft. McCoy was given a sudden change in mission, '...put up a fence or you won't be going home at the end of AT...' These guys put up about a bazillion linear feet of 10 foot high concertina wire topped fence and (then Camp McCoy) was suddenly turned into a Cuban boat person detention camp. The fence is long torn down but the facilities are still in place. The then hastily constructed World War II wood barracks, which have a maximum life cycle of 40 years, are still in good shape due to regular maintenance, and partly due to the sandy soil (absence of wood destroying insects)... The point is, if McCoy can be set up as a camp for Cubans, it can just as easily be set up as a camp for American patriots.

Money is constantly being dumped into this post in the way of new construction. The recently completed Wisconsin State Patrol Academy and the State Military Academy are examples. The state academy trains National Guard enlisted people to be officers through the OCS (Officer Candidate School) program. McCoy is a federal post used mostly to support the Reserve and Active armed forces components. Why are these two state entities on federal property?

Don't let me forget to mention that units of the (then) West

German (now) united German Army have been training at McCoy since the late 80s. Why McCoy? One of the so-called reasons given is that '...the local area has a lot of German-American people...' which is true. So what? Are they here to train or to look for long-lost relatives? As recently as the fall of 1995, I have seen a German flag flying outside of their barracks, a foreign flag flying on a U.S. military reservation. Go see for yourself. All of the aforementioned are easily verifiable.

— Also of note: Section 1065 of the February, 1995 Defense Authorization Act authorized the Army to conduct a demonstration project using civilian prison labor. This simply legalized civilian inmate labor programs which had already been going on at twelve army installations since 1989.

Currently, these facilities exist at Fort Bliss, Fort Dix, and Camp Atterbury. There are also eight non-resident programs (off-post) at Parks Reserve Forces Training Area, Red River Army Depot, Fort Lee, Fort McClellan, Fort Stewart, Fort McPherson, Fort Indian Town Gap, and Anniston Army Depot. These programs run between $263,000 and $3,500,000 yearly cost.

Many for-profit prison labor programs are already in place, such as the one at Ross Correctional Institution near Chillicothe, Ohio, where inmates are paid 35 cents and hour at the Honda plant in Marysville, Ohio — a rather significant wage undercutting from what union members are paid doing the same jobs. [29]

And, if there are not enough prisons in the country, the *Daily Oklahoman* reports, "Senator Jim Inhofe and Governor elect Frank Keating are considering a proposal to ship Oklahoma inmates to Mexican prisons to ease overcrowding in state prisons, the *McCurtain Daily Gazette* reported Thursday." [30]

Further confirmation of the burgeoning industry in creating detention camps comes from S.C., who posted the following message on the Internet:

I recently gave a bid to a company for some computer work. I did not get this bid and they have not returned my calls for obvious reasons, being a conflict of interest. Somehow they found out who

I was and decided it would not be in their best interest to allow me access to their data base. I must say, they are right. The company is called [name deleted]. The company is run by a man with whom I spoke several times. What they do is set up security systems for new detention camps. They just finished three in the Phoenix, Arizona area and are moving north now. [The owner] also told me they are working in Texas on one now and bid jobs all over the U.S. They do not advertise for obvious reasons and the owner is foreign born... I was hoping to get access to their files in order to be a little more detailed about their plans, however, it fell through. The owner also said they are very busy! — S.C. [31]

Another grass roots report: "I thought you might be interested in these pictures of one of two 'prison' buses I saw in Kentucky in December. What is unusual about these are: 1) they are unmarked — no prison name, or agency name anywhere, 2) they have federal government license plates, 3) they are white with a baby blue stripe at the top, which looks like a shadow in the photo, but isn't 4) it was driven by uniformed personnel with no visible insignia." [32]

Other detainment centers were originally built during World War II, and are allegedly renovated or are in the process of renovation. They include:

Opelika, Alabama; Florence, Arizona; Gila River, Arizona; Yuma, Arizona; Jerome, Arkansas; Rohwer, Arkansas; Manzanar, California; Tulelake, California; Grenada, Colorado; Trinidad, Colorado; Minipoka, Idaho; Concordia, Kansas; Livingston, Louisiana; Houlton, Maine; Scottsbluff, Nebraska; Mcalester, Oklahoma; Crossville, Tennessee; Mexia, Texas; Millard, Utah; and Hart Mountain, Wyoming. [33]

NOTES:

1. Holmes, Steven A, "U.S. Prisons Hold 1 Million," New York Times News Service; "Illegal Immigrants One-Fourth of Federal Prisoners," *The Populist Observer,* November 1993; "National News Briefs," *Patriot Report,* April 1996
2. Jefferson, M.W. America Under Siege. Freedom & Liberty Foundation, Knoxville, Tennessee, 1974

3. Blair, Mike, "Tidal Wave of Haitians Due; Arkansas Facility Prepared," *The Spotlight,* July 11, 1994; Jefferson
4. Jefferson
5. Ibid.
6. Ibid.
7. "New Prison/Hospital Found in Florida," *Patriot Report,* December, 1995
8. Anonymous report
9. Jefferson
10. Anonymous
11. Ibid.
12. Ibid.
13. Ibid.
14. Ibid.
15. Anonymous report from former Joint Chiefs of Staff source
16. Green, Jr., Harold R., Correspondence with the author
17. Anonymous; "Letters to the Editor," *Patriot Report,* July 1994; Jefferson
18. "Letters to the Editor, *Patriot Report,* February 1997
19. Jefferson
20. Blair, Mike, "Military Base to House U.S. Dissidents?," *The Spotlight,* October 10, 1994
21. Anonymous military source
22. Ibid.
23. "New Fed Prison Run By Australians," *Patriot Report,* May, 1997
24. Jefferson
25. Thompson, Jeff, Undated correspondence with the author
26. Jefferson
27. "News Briefs and National Rumors," *Patriot Report,* July 1994
28. "FEMA Prison Completed, But Who Will Be the Prisoners?", *Patriot Report,* March 1997
29. Smith, Mark, "Army to Use Inmate Civilian Labor," *The Free American,* January 1997; Solidarity, published by the United Auto Workers, undated clipping in author's possession; Jefferson
30. "Plan Reported to Ship Inmates to Mexico," *Daily Oklahoman,* December 23, 1994
31. Internet posting, November 12, 1996
32. "Letters to the Editor," *Patriot Report,* April 1997
33. Jefferson

12

VITAL SIGNS:

THE QUADRANT SIGN CODE

Researcher Harold R. Green, Jr. has been studying the reflective stickers that have been placed on the back of road signs around the nation. These stickers are widely alleged to incorporate a secret code that will be used during a New World Order takeover in directing foreign troops who do not understand English to their destinations in the U.S.

For my part, I believe that Mr. Green has made a breakthrough in proving that this code exists, and in deciphering its meaning. My guess is that the authorities who are planning on using this code are going to be rather perturbed when they learn that it is no longer a secret, and that its meaning will now be disseminated around the world. Mr. Green's report, edited for length, is reprinted here with his permission:

Basic "Clipped" Sticker Codes

After nearly two years of studying the code system on our signs here in Michigan, it is my thought that the "clipped" stickers, or "TAC-MARKS" as I believe they are called, probably originated from the eight-sided geometric octagon or stop sign. By dividing a stop sign into quarters, one can clearly see the four sections (squares) with their respective "CLIPPED" corner missing. Here, right before us, are the four Tac-Marks used in the basic secret code!

From this the designated routes and facility locations were set-up into a cleverly devised code system only known by a select group who will carry out their missions, probably under martial law. This stop sign also holds the keys to the new, rectangular, dated M.DOT (Michigan Department of Transportation) stickers. The "Clip" is key to the Tac-Mark coding system.

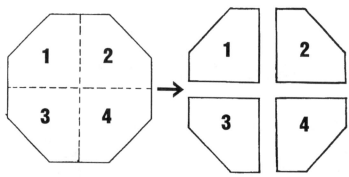

I have numbered each of the segments to identify them better as each one is a particular component to the code system. I started observing consistent patterns involving segments #1 and #2 as I approached important turns and intersections. These seemed to precede these points without exception and led me to believe them to be related to turns in some way. Segments #3 and #4 many times accompanied #1 and #2, and at other times seemed to appear alone at some side roads. It became very apparent that these clipped reflective stickers were definitely some type of directional markers.

I finally made an important discovery when I happened upon a facility with a LARGE BLUE marker clipped on the upper-right corner at the "Shawono Center" detention facility near Grayling, Michigan. Believing this to be the end of the trail, I decided to work my way backwards to see what stickers were used at the various turns and corners leading to Shawono. This ultimately led me to the cracking of the Tac-Mark hidden code system.

The UPPER-LEFT and UPPER-RIGHT clipped markers are both TURN INDICATORS. They seem to be used interchangeably, though the UPPER-LEFT clipped marker is used primarily on state and interstate highways. These normally do not show direction, but signal an up-coming turn ahead.

The LOWER-LEFT and LOWER-RIGHT clipped markers are directional, or POINTERS. They POINT in the direction that the turn is to be made, or are used to direct your field of vision to the opposite side of the roadway to other signs for further information. I call these types of pointers CROSS-OVERS.

The above is the consistent BASIC CODE for the Tac-Mark system. Color or size of the marker does not alter this code. For example, Shawono Center, a detention facility, has a LARGE, reflective, BLUE upper-right Tac-Mark on the facility signs. These are TURN INDICATORS. Regardless of these factors the code is the same.

When I was first made aware of the Tac-Mark on the signs here in Michigan, some alert citizens had already been questioning the Michigan Department of Transportation as to markers on the backs of the road signs. The response was a collection of absurdities that bordered on the laughable, to plain utter nonsense! Here are a few of them:

"What reflective markers?"

"Oh, those are for the snow-plows, so they won't hit the signs!"

"Well, we are testing paint to see how it withstands weathering."

"We are testing a new adhesive, to see how long it takes them to fall off."

"Those markers are for chemical and hazardous haulers to follow."

You would think these folks would compare notes before they open their lying mouths. Such response flies in the face of common sense and shows what little regard our government officials have for the truth and for the citizens who finance their fat paychecks. The Department of Transportation, under mounting pressure, finally had to come up with a lie that they could all tell in unison, and fool the public enough to get them off their backs. At last, a statement was made that seemed fairly reasonable, and yet would allow them to continue with their plans and still cover up what they were really doing. They apologized for all the confusion and stated, "We are dating the road signs." They even came up with proof! A new sticker was then produced that actually had dated borders that would be punched out on the appropriate date by M.Dot employees putting up the signs. The truth is, I can take them to specific signs that have absolutely no punches on the markers at all, and I can also take them to signs I know were put up over three years ago, and yet, have last year's date punched out on them! It is all a total fraud and an absolute waste of taxpayer's money, not to mention the real intent behind it all, which would make many of our government officials guilty of treason and sedition if the facts were brought out and those responsible prosecuted.

Below, you will plainly see what I discovered about the "new" dated M.Dot markers. The deception is clever, but the code is basically the same as the Tac-Mark system. As they started phasing out many of the Tac-Marks and phasing in the new dated M.Dot, I began to see patterns emerging and similarities dealing with what appeared to be a CONVERSION PROCESS. I took over a hundred photos and spread them out before me, and painstakingly began searching for keys to unlock the riddle. By God's grace, and prayer, I began to see the code system unfold. The keys were the relationship between the CLIPPED CORNERS of the Tac-Marks and the new M.Dot's PLACEMENT in the different quadrants of the signs.

Code Conversion/New Dated M.Dot Stickers

The new dated M.Dot sticker code is actually a blown-up version of the Tac-Mark code only using the QUADRANT of the sign instead of the CLIPPED CORNER of the sticker. It is best illustrated by going back to the STOP SIGN. Divide it mentally into four sections. The UPPER-LEFT quadrant of a STOP SIGN has a "clipped" UPPER LEFT corner just like the UPPER-LEFT clipped TAC-MARK. This TAC-MARK is a TURN INDICATOR. That means that if one of the new dated M.DOT stickers is placed in the UPPER-LEFT QUADRANT of a STOP SIGN, it also becomes a TURN INDICATOR.

Likewise, with each clipped sticker, there is a corresponding quadrant that matches its code. Very clever! This is the case with any type of sign; just divide it into four sections and check which quadrant the sticker appears in, then decode it:

(1) UPPER-LEFT is the TURN INDICATOR quadrant.
(2) UPPER-RIGHT is also a TURN INDICATOR quadrant.
(3) LOWER-LEFT is a LEFT DIRECTIONAL POINTER.
(4) LOWER-RIGHT DIRECTIONAL POINTER.

I have named this QUADRANT SIGN ENCODATION.

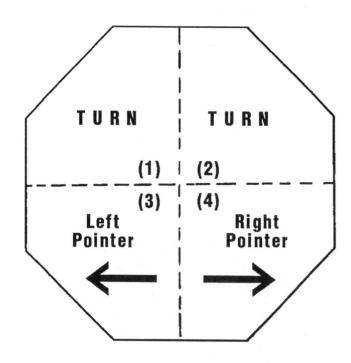

KAIKASKA "County" MARKER

Examples of Quadrant Sign Encodation

Upper-Left Turn Indicator ⟶

Many times is turned upside down. Also is found on the back of signs with arrows. These DO NOT show direction, but indicated that a turn of some kind is to be made.

Upper-Right Turn Indicator ⟶

This is used less often than than the above, but it serves the same purpose. Also has been in the upside down position.

Lower-Left Directional Pointer ⟶

These are used in conjunction with the turn indicators. They "point" in the direction of the turn, or are used to transfer attention to other signs and information on the opposite side of the road

Lower-Right Directional Pointer ⟶

As the above, the code reveals the direction you are to go or "look." Without these it is impossible to follow your route or: facility location.

Note: This is primarily dealing with center-mounted signs. There are some variations when two posts are used which will be presented later.

Other Turn Indicators/Pointers ⟶

This configuration is a TURN HERE indicator. Note the M.DOT marker placed "on its end." This is another type of turn indicator. Here it is used in conjunction with a LOWER-RIGHT QUAD-RANT pointer. You will find this usually

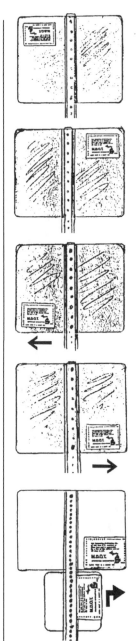

Sketches by H. R. Green, Jr.

on the left side of the roadway just before a designated right turn, or pointing directly into a facility entrance.

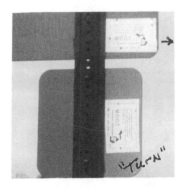
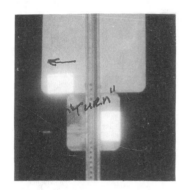

Two-Posted Signs/Code

The two-posted signs also use the QUADRANT SIGN ENCODING method (see page 174). The only real variation is the center-line turn position. When the marker appears midway between the posts, it signals an upcoming turn. It may move vertically on the center line and still remain a "turn indicator." Also, all diamond-shaped signs hold the same characteristics. Center-line HORIZONTAL movement, right or left, sometimes will indicate the turn ahead will be to the right or left. These signs also make good "cross-overs."

The NO PASSING triangle signs (right) are used extensively as "pointers." If the marker appears on either side of the outside posts, the whole sign becomes an arrowhead pointer or cross-over. Again, it is is a two-post sign, the M.DOT marker positioned between them makes it a TURN INDICATOR.

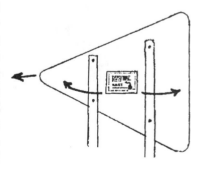

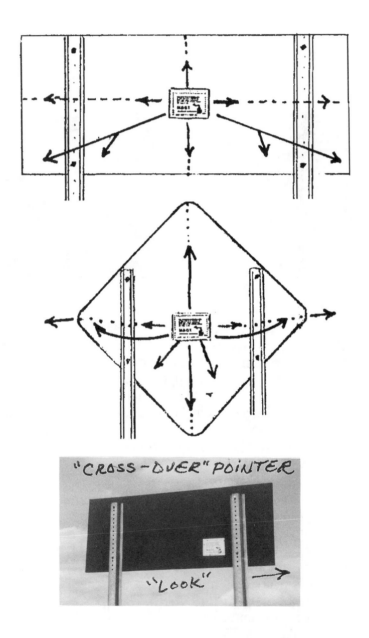

Two-posted signs using the Quadrant Sign Encoding Method.

The Discovery of the "Facility Symbol"

I personally interviewed an employee of the Kalkaska M.DOT, who has worked for them for 38 years. He stated to me that their department has not stickered or erected any permanent signs on the highways for over seven years. He said "special crews" have taken over all such work. This means, not only has the stickering been done by this firm, but the erecting also. This explains the strange and ridiculous stacking of road signs in recent years. For example, check out the photo on page 158. The "Prison Area" sign is for the Shawono Center detention facility west of Grayling, in Crawford County, Michigan/ Last spring (1996), the WEST M-72 sign, which was standing about 1/4 mile down the road, was pulled up and "stacked" on the upper-left corner of the "Prison Area" sign for some strange reason. Was it really that strange? Not if you check the back of the signs. When I put a spotlight beam on the back I found three M.DOT stickers "stacked" on the lower-right corner of each sign. I would find this SYMBOL at every important marked facility here in northern Michigan. I have henceforth named it the "FACILITY SYMBOL." It is apparent that this STACK-ING is done to "build" their markers with the lie that they are dating their signs. (see page 176)

Geometric Shapes/Facility Symbols
"Cluster Sign Decoding"

It is one thing to follow a route using the revealed code rules on individual signs but it is another thing when you come to a "wall" of signs plastered with stickers that don't seem to make any sense at all! Many times, hidden in these "clusters" of signs, are GEOMETRIC SHAPES and DESIGNS. This is where the individual stickers are placed in a configuration on pre-arranged signs that show direction of turns, or entrances to an important facility. These sticker placements many times violate the "code rules." I believe this is done to throw off any would-be detective trying to break into their codes.

Stacked signs found near important marked facilities, such as this Army Aviation Support Facility in Northern Michigan.

The main objective here is to "build" the geometric designs. If it violates any code rules it is to their advantage. In the following photos you will notice some familiar shapes. Notice also that the shapes are in triads (threes). These are "facility symbols." Every major facility noted for confiscation that I have found has been marked with one of these triad symbols. The arrangement of these route signs have been conveniently positioned to create two types of geometric shapes. The facility here is the Grayling Army Airfield and helicopter pads. Note the geometric "ARROWHEAD" design used on the back of the northbound road signs pointing directly into the gate of the facility. On the southbound signs you will find a different geometric design, a broken arrow, or what I call a "DOG LEG" pointer. This was done I believe on purpose to not establish a pattern (see page 178).

It is important to state again that there is a difference between reading individual signs when following a route, and "Cluster Sign Decoding." Cluster signs appear just before an upcoming intersection where directional information is needed concerning routes, cities, miles, and facilities. Remember, hidden within the many stickers at these signs are the "Facility Symbols" and "Geometric Designs." In the following photos you will see combinations being used to show the direction of a facility or facilities. Note, both a FACILITY SYMBOL and LOWER-LEFT DIRECTIONAL POINTER are used to make a GEOMETRIC ARROWHEAD (top photo, page 179). This means that there is an important facility or facilities in the direction indicated. Also notice a geometric ARCHED ARROW formed by three (triad) stickers, pointing in the same direction. The lower photo shows another array of the same "shapes" but notice the trickery. The stickers appear to be sloppily placed as if to show that they were just haphazardly stuck there! Not so! Notice the two stickers standing on their ends. M.DOT markers on their ends are TURN INDICATORS. These are made to appear as mistakes as you see the other stickers are all slightly off kilter, or tilted. This clever use of pre-arranged signs and symbols are used consistently everywhere in our state.

North and southbound cluster signs containing "facility symbols," pointing directly to the gate of the Grayling Army Airfield.

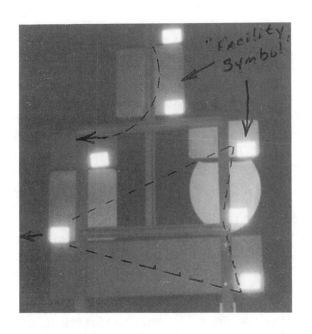

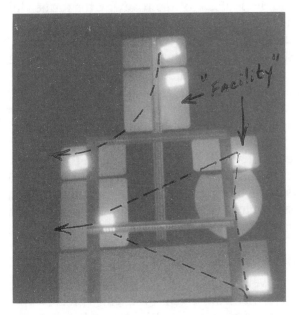

Cluster signs usually appear just before an upcoming intersection where directional information is needed.

Decoding a Route: Which Way Do We Go?

One of the creepiest feelings is to drive down the road and see all of these stickers and know what they mean and to be able to follow where they are going. Here are some general rules I have learned over the past year that have opened up the ability to follow a ROUTE to the destination.

To follow a route to a destination, you begin decoding the signs on the RIGHT side of the roadway with the regular direction of the traffic. (Note: During martial law no-one will be allowed on the roadway except "authorized vehicles." These vehicles will be able to travel in any direction, uninhibited.) Each sign must be read over your right shoulder. This is why I feel when the time comes "they" will have both a driver and a "spotter" with a light to illuminate the backs of the signs.

Be especially alert for "cross-overs." These could be lower-right quadrant "pointers," or two posted rectangular signs with the M.DOT sticker to the right of center. These direct your field of vision to the left side of the roadway for further information on the backs of the signs to your left.

Watch for TURN INDICATORS followed by a series of POINTERS. Many times these pointers will zig-zag across the roadway just before a turn. The backs of many of the signs are COLOR CODED, some are yellow, some green, also brown and black. You match your back colors from side-to-side.

At important intersections, watch the sign "clusters" for facility symbols, geometric shapes such as dog-leg pointers, arrows, etc. They will be there, and make the appropriate turn.

Although this is all very intriguing, the real point is that our highways ARE being coded, and the Michigan Department of Transportation has been lying through their teeth about the real intent of their statewide operations concerning these stickers.

Watch the Public Schools

In my travels through some of the small cities and towns here in Northern Michigan, I kept observing a recurring Tac-Mark configuration. This was a GREEN marker above a WHITE marker. When I discovered the code system for the Tac-Marks, it became quite clear what this array of markers was all about. These markers are for the future HUMAN PROCESSING CENTERS. I know this because I work at one! It is the local public school. When driving by these "green over white" markers, I noticed I was in a SCHOOL ZONE, or the Tac-Marks were pointing down a road that led directly to a school.

In Bill Clinton's Goals 2000, every public school will be globalized into the Internet Jungle before the turn of the century. This has become quite evident at the school where I am employed. During the Christmas break our public school was "laced" with the latest high tech computer hook-ups, Internet, and fiber optics. There are module receptacles in literally every room but the restrooms. There is even what could be described as an "indoctrination room" where there are no less than eight 36 and 40 inch view screens with four video cameras with zoom lenses, and specially mounted microphones in the ceiling tiles. All of which is connected to a central control center 20 miles away where it is linked up to every school in the country, and most likely, the world! It would not be far-fetched to easily convert any public school facility into a processing center or even a detention facility for dissidents not cooperating with the New Order that is planned by the year 2000. Whatever the case, watch the public schools, for they are marked by the DOT for some special program during the dismantling of our nation.

[For questions, comments, or further information, please contact by mail: "Free In-Deed Researchers," Attn: H.R. Green, Jr., Post Office Box 175, Fife Lake, Michigan 49633]

13

THE END OF AMERICA

A rigid system of elitist control is in force today on this planet, and with the advent of new technology for control, the prospects for America and mankind have never looked more bleak. We are outwitted before our birth, set upon a game grid where checkmate is the pre-determined outcome. We are channeled through economic and social determinants that we deal with little better than a lab rat controls its destiny in an experimental maze.

While humanity is in continual economic lockdown, additional controls are liberally applied, through television, through the news, through the manipulation of event and societal structure. This keeps the human species more confused, more deluded and sidetracked into dead-end religions, drugs, fashions, and fears. The citizen, beset by various troubles and prevented from understanding his situation, does not see the interlocking controls and utilization that dictate most of his actions.

Is this a paranoid interpretation of life, of history? I don't think so. And I believe that a survey of the activities of the controllers, of elitist intentions carried out by a host of governments, secret societies, intelligence agencies, and crime cabals will bear out this grim assessment.

Robert Anton Wilson has wondered, "And why is it that we all know the word 'paranoid,' but hardly anybody can think of words for rational suspicion or rational fear — even though both of these would appear necessary for survival in a world where every major government has a secret police agency and every corporation and political party has a 'dirty tricks' department?"

Point well taken.

Gazing at the chaos that America has become, one sees the

science fictional world of Burgess' *Clockwork Orange* synthesized with a decadent Rome. Unemployment runs at 15% or more (regardless of the government's "adjusted" figures), while the country is saddled with a national debt so huge as to be unpayable. Taxation and licensing fees consume 80% of real spending power, forcing husband, wife, and sometimes children to work, destroying any semblance of family life. Literacy levels among school children are at an all-time low, and education primarily concerns itself with destroying individuality, and preparing children for life as workers in the hive. Crime runs rampant and is promoted as a fashion statement by the media.

At this time, the United States is the recipient for more illegal immigrants than all other countries combined, flooding the country with a surplus of labor and a surfeit of need. When it is whispered that unchecked immigration may be having a negative influence on the quality of life in America, the protester is tarred with the epithet of "racist."

The issue is not one of race, but is cultural and economic. Allowing millions of uneducated persons across our borders, persons who do not speak the primary language of this country, is custom-created to induce chaos. Other problems fostered by illegal immigration are the spread of disease bred in poverty, and the huge burden placed upon welfare and social services. There is an overall increase in crime of all sorts, with a large percentage of it perpetrated by groups like the Yakuza, the Jamaican "posses," Mexican drug gangs, and others.

Rice University economist Dr. Donald Huddle documents that illegal aliens are taking America to the cleaners to the tune of $13 billion dollars a year. That is a very modest estimate, although the real damage cannot be fully gauged in terms of the buck. [1]

The toleration of illegal immigration is an effective weapon of the New World Order for destroying American sovereignty. It paves the way for the global plantation, in which the labor of millions is monopolized for the benefit of the few who own the engines of production. This is not a mysterious process, although politicians do their best to obfuscate what is going on.

Although there would be no great problem in limiting illegal immigration, these mostly unskilled workers are desired by big business in order to maintain a huge labor pool demanding only minimum wage. They also serve as a prod for other workers: rock the boat or complain about wages or conditions and there will be a hundred other workers to take your place.

Illegal immigration is useful in demoralizing the American citizen. Americans are used to a degree of freedom, and expect it. Having this view, they are almost certainly seen as a threat to the New World Order. Illegal immigration is being used as a weapon against America, gradually reducing the standard of living into a parity with the Third World. It is a means of reducing resistance.

As the final consolidation of the New World Order takes place, as the control mechanisms of the United States are handed over to the U.N. and its subsidiary internationalist bodies, there will be those who object — object to any number of activities, such as gun grabs, biodiversity migrations, U.N. troops, or Russian tanks in the back garden.

There may even be an effective resistance movement to these activities. This resistance, the internationalists insist, must be eliminated, and are putting in place the mechanisms for doing so.

There does not even have to be a head-on assault by black choppers, where U.N. blue helmets battle it out with American patriots over acreage in Tennessee. Due to the careful, effective planning of the New World Order, it will probably not be necessary.

Per the long term Fabian plan and slogan, "Proceed slowly," most machinations of the New World Order will continue to take place in Congress, and in groups like the Trilateral Commission, the Bilderbergers, and the Council on Foreign Relations. These changes will take place over the next generation or so, without uproar except in the underground press. Day by day the American standard of living will slip away, but most will not notice. Even if they do, they will not believe they have the ability to do anything about it.

The New World Order controllers, so far as I can tell, are not anxious for a confrontation. Confrontations boldly draw the battle lines, allowing people to see what is going on. They render the situation in black and white, instead of deepening shades of gray, and make clear the opposition of average Americans to globalist intervention.

On the other hand, the black choppers provide for an effective response if and when Americans do wake up to the dismantling of their country. If a sudden offensive is mounted against the patriot or populist movement in the U.S., then the initial strikeforce will be probably be the black helicopters. These maneuverable tactical craft, which can be utilized in urban settings, and equipped with massive firepower, can quickly mop up hotspots of patriotic resistance.

FEMA will no doubt coordinate this final goal. A sudden onslaught of black choppers will capture or kill dissidents to the New World Order, and will be used to patrol cities and transport troublemakers to the concentration camps.

The black choppers, however, may never be utilized on such a nationwide scale. America may go down without a whimper, believing that safe chains are preferable to the insecurities of freedom. On the other hand, it may not go that way, either.

In April of 1997 information was received from a former CIA microbiologist named Larry Harris, the author of *Bacteriological Warfare, A Major Threat to North America*. Harris had been contacted by intelligence agents who met with him after being involved with an operation taking place at the Iowa State University, in Ames, Iowa. On February 6, the American intelligence agents had detained seven Iraqi women implicated in a plot to release anthrax and plague virus into the population. Taken to medical facilities, the women were searched and found to be carrying vials of viral agents in their vaginas. These agents are deadly within a matter of days if not treated with antibiotics; of course, in a situation of country-wide infection, antibiotic supplies would be depleted almost instantly. Found at other locations were cultures for growing viruses. Harris, who obtained additional information from an Iraqi woman, says that there is a plan to wage biological warfare on America, and the first attack will take place within the next few years — before 2002. The woman confided to him that simultaneous strikes with anthrax and bubonic plague would take place at 100 locations in the United States. [2]

Not to worry. Given an event of the above magnitude, FEMA would step right in to handle the situation, to handle it terminatedly. Meanwhile, government officials will be playing checkers and watching videos in their plush underground bunkers.

NOTES:

1. *New York Times,* December 8, 1995; "U.S. Prepares for Millions Fleeing Mexico," *Patriot Report,* March 1996; "Illegal Aliens Destroying Our Country," *The Spotlight,* April 11, 1994
2. "Iraqi Women in U.S. Found With Vials of Deadly Anthrax & Plague," *Wake-Up Call America,* 1997

14

ENDGAME STRATEGY

Beyond the manipulations of the globalists, another strategic checkmate awaits America. We have been told that since the Fall and Winter of 1989 the Soviet Union is toast, that Russia has liberalized, and that we may breath a sigh of relief. If we do it may be the last breath we take.

Before I give specifics of the checkmate, I would like to discuss information that is mentioned little in the dominant publications and newscasts in this country.

These media outlets, one for one, promote the view that the Cold War is over. They say that Russia is a military castrato, and that all the American people have to do is sit back and wait for the captains of industry and politics to steward this planet into a utopia of unforeseen pleasures and security. I don't believe that is how it is going to shake down.

It is not surprising that the U.S. would see the new era in Russian politics as a sudden outbreak of peace. Western media relies, in large part, for its information about what happens in the former Soviet Union on the ITAR-Tass news agency, and the newer Interfax, an organization centered in Moscow, but with the Western headquarters in Denver. Interfax is allegedly staffed with twenty KGB agents. The idea that Communism is over, in short, appears to be disinformation.

Soviet defector Oleg Kalugin, a former director of the KGB against Western intelligence organizations, indicates that 55 Western intelligence agencies have been deeply infiltrated by the KGB/GRU. Also, due to liberalized immigration and visitation, America is wide-open to the penetration of KGB, GRU, and Spetsnaz agents.

The Spetsnaz are something to behold. They are trained in

Russia as commandos, and are skilled in attacking communications centers, water and power stations, airfields, and other areas vital to national interests. Spetsnaz are accustomed to wearing the uniforms of other countries, of the U.S., NATO, or the U.N. and are trained in NATO command phrases. They are deliberately trained in brutal conditions, and are reportedly forced to kill live prisoners, and swim through underground tunnels filled with decaying corpses to accustom and to harden them.

An intelligence analyst informs us that, "Many [Spetsnaz] are living as civilians in Western countries (including the U.S.) while others come as tourists and students to familiarize themselves with the countries and customs of those Western countries to which they will be assigned." Estimates place 50,000 Soviet intelligence agents operating in America today. [1]

According to intelligence analysts, the Russian Mafia is in fact a creation and a cover for KGB/GRU activities. Former Polish Ambassador Zdzislaw Rurarz has fingered the GRU, saying that "gangsters" are trained and employed by the GRU for "wet sanctions," i.e. assassinations, and then sent across the world their duties to perform.

Russian collaboration with criminal elements is not difficult to believe. The Communists have worked in collaboration with the American wing of the Mafia for many years. Maurice Malkin, a formerly high-level member of the Communist Party, U.S.A., and one-time managing editor for the *Daily Worker,* revealed that,

> The Communist Party of the United States has had an agreement with the Mafia since 1924, with the arrival in the United States of Eneo Sormenti, alias Vidali Contreras Victorio... Upon his arrival he re-established the understanding between the Mafia and the Communists that was made in Italy by Bordiga, a leader of the Italian Communist Party, and by Ercoli Palmieri Togliatti, alias Ercoli.
>
> The agreement called for the Mafia to do work for the Communist International, such as murdering opponents, distributing counterfeit currency and dope, stealing government documents such

as seals and stamps for foreign passports, and other jobs that Communist agents could not carry out, but that the Mafia and its connections could." [2]

Russians penetrate — without the need for secrecy — the highest levels of the American military, as illustrated by an anecdote of Colonel Jim Ammerman, a 26-year veteran of the CIA and the Green Berets. Ammerman states, "The officer, the four star general that is in charge over U.S. Army, U.S. forces Europe, his name is Joulwan... He has two deputies, people who can act on his behalf if he's not present at the moment. One of them is a three-star American, and one of them is a three-star Russian. And he was in the most classified, top secret building that we have on the continent of Europe. I've been there, I had a son-in-law in the infantry, a colonel, and I visited him on active duty with a top secret clearance. For me to get in to see him he had to come to the door, and he signed for me, both of us being in uniform. I had to be in his sight during the entire time that I was in that highly classified building. Now we have a Russian in there who knows all the secrets that we have, specifically all our secrets that pertain to Europe, to Eastern Europe and to Russia. I say something is rotten in Denmark." [3]

Although glasnost/perestroika is heralded as the New Age in international relations, it is never, never mentioned that this is the sixth period of disengagement between Russia and the Americans since 1920. All of these "thaws" in American/Soviet relations have ended in renewed hostilities.

Alexander Solzhenitsyn warned on Moscow television, "Communism has by no means collapsed... Don't forget through all this, the structure of the KGB has been retained... The KGB remains a large force with a large apparatus and long far-reaching tentacles."

Russia is regenerating its former empire, as I suspect it had always planned. The previous head of the KGB is now president in Azerbaijan. Bulgaria's prime minister is the "former" Communist Zhan Videnov. In Hungary, "former" Communist Gyula Horn is now president. Lithuania is now run by the former First Secretary of the Lithuanian Communist Party.

Poland is run by more "former" Communists. Romania's president is Ion Illiescu, the former Romanian Communist Central Committee Secretary. Slobodan Milosevit, the Chairman of the Serbian Communist Party, is now president in that country. "Former" Communists run Slovokia.

For all the talk about starving troops and the sell-off of their military equipment, Russia still has the largest soldiering force in the world. It also possesses an estimated strikeforce of 12-45,000 nuclear ICBMs (depending upon the analyst asked). These multiple-warhead missiles are more than adequate to incinerate America, and there is absolutely nothing to counter them once they are launched.

A declassified report written in 1992, the year that Russia supposedly totally collapsed, documents that 55 percent of the country's budget was spent on the military — whereas the figure announced to the world was 12 percent. Russian industry continues to produce huge quantities of armaments (estimated by some observers as 6-7 times the quantity publicly announced).

At the same time that Russia has "fallen behind" in reduction of Strategic Arms Reduction Treaty agreements, Defense Secretary William Perry warns, America is rapidly working to reduce its stockpile of nuclear ICBMS, first to 2,000 missiles, and then to as few as 100. [4]

While Russian military force is remaining on even keel, or increasing, America has reduced its troop strength in Europe from 400,000 troops stationed there in the 1980s, to less than 100,000 today. Numbers of American troops in Europe are planned to be downsized literally to nothing over the next few years.

The American press is oddly silent about the reform in Russian military strategy since the beginning of their "open arms" policy toward America. Still, something occasionally leaks out. As documented in a 1993 story in the *Chicago Tribune*, Russia has "adopted a first strike nuclear policy." This means that the Russians are willing to fire the first nuclear shots at America, and to watch the world go up in smoke. [5]

Major General George J. Keegan, Jr., an expert on Russian defense, states that the Kremlin believes, as they have always believed, that the Russian people will survive a nuclear war. One of the reasons for this is that the Russians have long placed emphasis in their military spending on civil defense, a concern that the American government has never particularly had, other than in the building of massive underground bunkers for the leaders of government.

Keegan states that, "We examined thirty-nine of the largest cities and found that every apartment house built after 1955 had a massive nuclear bomb shelter in the basement. Secondly, we found large tunnels interconnecting every one of these buildings. And in these tunnels, we found water, electric power conduits, and a vast storage of medical supplies: hospital-type facilities."

Also found by American satellite photographic analysts are 75 huge underground defense complexes in Russia. "How big are they?" Major General Keegan asks. "Roughly the size of the Pentagon. How deep were they? They were completely covered and were underground. Filled and covered with what? One, with 100 feet of reinforced concrete and 400 feet of earth fill. That's two or three times the strength of the Hoover Dam. Not one, but seventy five. A number of them had large steel stairs covered with concrete. The giant shelters contain storage tanks for water and for diesel fuel to power generators. Many of them were very posh, landscaped, with beautiful barracks around them." [6]

Not one with undue concern for American security, President Clinton is eagerly pushing to include Eastern Bloc countries into NATO, in my view compromising the organization with Communist membership. Although certain Soviet leaders have complained about the entry of these countries into NATO, methinks they protest too much. Russians are historically the best chess players in the world.

While America has curtailed its production of submarines to two subs manufactured every six years, the Russians will produce 35 subs during that same period. By the year 2000,

Russia will have 122 nuclear attack subs, almost three times as many as the U.S. According to *Defense News*, the Russians are upgrading sea-based weapons, and are building "an extremely fast rocket-powered torpedo that has no equivalent in the U.S. or other Western Navies." Also being built is, "a new type of anti-ship cruise missile that would be launched from the torpedo tubes of future submarines and the Oscar II cruise missile-carrying submarine." [7]

At the beginning of 1996, one or more Russian Akula-class nuclear attack submarines were spotted in Puget Sound, off the state of Washington, and in the Strait of Juan de Fuca, separating Washington state from Vancouver Island, British Columbia. The mission of these undersea prowlers is alleged to be the charting of northern coastal waters. Other Russian subs have been seen off the coast of Georgia and in the Gulf of Mexico. There are reports of a secret Russian submarine base in Cuba.[8]

Russia is engaged in many secret military projects that, as I learn about them, undermine my sense of glorious perestroika. As noted in the the Medford, Oregon *Mail Tribune:*

> In a secret project that may have roots deep in the Cold War, Russia is building a mammoth, underground military complex in the Ural Mountains. The project which has been observed by U.S. spy satellites, involves a huge complex served by a railroad, a highway and thousands of workers. The construction of the project mystifies American specialists who speculate that it may be anything from an underground nuclear command post to a secret weapons production plant, the report said. The Russian Defense ministry refused to discuss the project." [9]

Another secret weapons projects in Russia was revealed in 1991, when Vil Mirzayanov, a 57-year-old Russian scientist, blew the whistle on a chemical weapons program that he had been working on at Moscow State Union Scientific Research Institute for Chemistry and Technology since 1965.

According to Mirzayanov, the institute was engaged in creating chemical weapons, and "the greatest results [at the institute] were achieved between 1985 and 1991... During that time, our laboratories created Substance A-230, a weapon about which I can only say that its killing efficiency surpassed any known military toxin by a factor of five to eight."

Another chemical weapon produced at the facility was called FT, and its entire purpose was to blow away whole populations. FT was tested in Afghanistan in the early 1980s, where Mirzayanov says the water sources of entire towns were poisoned. Since FT leaves no traces in the body, the KGB, who sponsored the Afghanistan murders, knew there was no danger of detection.

Other weapons were developed at the institute, including "Novichok," a poison that is absorbed directly through the skin. Novichok is ten times more deadly than the most deadly nerve gas ever previously created.

Mirzayanov has mentioned another development, "the synthesis of a binary weapon based on Substance A-232, a toxin similar to A-230. This new weapon, part of the ultra-lethal 'Novichok' class, provides an opportunity for the military establishment to disguise production of components of binary weapons as common agricultural chemicals. Because the West does not know the formula its inspectors cannot identify the compounds."

As glasnost was declared by Mikhail Gorbachev in 1987, the institute continued to synthesize and test a wide variety of deadly chemical weapons. Mirzayanov notes that when a list of chemical weapons was submitted to the government, prior to Boris Yeltsin signing the Chemical Weapons Convention, the whole arsenal of poisons, including Novichok and FT, were not included in the list.

After his public statements, Mirzayanov was arrested by the KGB, but because of a campaign by groups in the West he was released. Recent reports say that Mirzyanov would like to present his case in the West about the continuing production of deadly chemical warfare agents, but his application for a passport has been denied on the basis of his knowledge of state secrets. [10]

According to the London *Sunday Times,* Russia is engaged

in developing other biowarfare weapons, including, "a super plague for which the West has no antidote." The paper says that "the work was being carried out in defiance of President Boris Yeltsin, who has been misled into believing the research has been halted. The *Sunday Times* said the plague that Russia is developing, in breach of international agreements, is so powerful that 440 pounds sprayed from planes or using airburst bombs could kill 500,000 people. The paper said a defector from the Bioperarat project told British intelligence last autumn of the steps that the Russian military had taken to keep the program going behind Yeltsin's back." [11]

Commentator Donald S. McAlvany astutely observes, "It is worth noting that the 1,000 or more new Russian military trucks being stored at a depot on federal land in the Desoto National Forest near Saucier, Mississippi... are designed for battlefield use during chemical, biological, or nuclear war. Why are they there?" [12]

In September 1996, the *London Sunday Times* released information in a secret Soviet military document that Pavel Grachev, the former defense minister, had ordered the activation of "Project Vulcan." This was the code phrase for research into a "strategic techtonic weapon," i.e. the use of underground nuclear weapons to unleash earthquakes and tidal waves on enemies. The *Sunday Times* further noted that money was still being funneled into Project Vulcan. Other information revealed that in 1987, just as perestroika was supposedly beginning, research had been approved on the logistics of setting off quakes along the San Andreas fault in California. [13]

The truth about Russia is something entirely different than what one reads in the newspapers, and the same is true of China, that long time Communist "enemy" of Russia. This is confirmed by the *New York Times* magazine: "While most countries in the world are cutting back, China has raised its published military budget by 75 percent since 1988, after adjusting for inflation. And the published budget vastly underestimates reality. It does not even include weapons procurement.

"The real figure is probably something like $20 billion,

which when adjusted for purchasing power may buy as much as a $100 billion defense budget in the West.'' The Stockholm International Peace Research Institute, on the other hand, says that China's military budget is at least six times the announced figure of $7.5 billion. [14]

Analysts say that the Chinese have been working on developing miniaturized nuclear bombs, and otherwise upgrading their nuclear capacity. One way in which they have been doing this was revealed in 1996, when the Ukrainian government fired two investigators at the Yuzhnoye Aerospace facility in the Ukraine. These men had made the mistake of reporting that they had caught Chinese agents red-handed in an attempt to steal plans for the SS-18 ICBM multiple warhead rocket. The Chinese, in fact, were not stealing the plans, but had bought them from the Ukrainians.

The Chinese are building up missile forces capable of hitting the U.S. by adapting Ukrainian SS-18 technology to Chinese DF-5 Chinese ICBMs. They are also building SS-18-style launchers, which will enable them to target 150 U.S. cities with nuclear bombs by the turn of the century, upgrading from the 10 U.S. cities now fixed in the atomic crosshairs. China is supporting its production of the SS-18 by selling the missiles to Iraq, Libya, and other nations. [15]

There is a game of international chess, played for life and death stakes, happening right under our noses. Closed due to cuts in military spending, a Long Beach, California Navy base is being leased to COSCO, a 600-vessel fleet shipping company owned wholly by the Chinese government. This is taking place with the approval of the Navy, although, according to former CIA director Robert Gates, ''without a national security review.''

COSCO has been operating through the naval yard for some time, and is not required to file written ship manifests declaring its cargo. It is estimated that only one out of 80 cargo containers are opened for inspection at the Long Beach base. [16]

The deal for the Long Beach naval yard was ushered along by the Clinton White House, but more specifically, by Bill

Clinton. Clinton and six members of Congress, including Senator Dianne Feinstein, Senator Barbara Boxer, and Representative Nancy Pelosi, were earlier warned by the FBI that Red China was going to be making contributions to them. Curious, isn't it, that all of the above-named approved of the Long Beach naval base deal? Also notable is that Senator Feinstein's husband, Richard Blum, is the managing director of an investment firm that is a consultant to COSCO, and that Blum has large investments in Red China. Bill Clinton is also alleged to have large secret Chinese holdings. [17]

Clinton has twice met with Long Beach officials to encourage the closing of the deal, which involves the turning the Navy base over to the city of Long Beach, with the city in turn leasing the base to COSCO, a part of the Chinese Ministry of Transportation. Also, the Clinton administration's Department of Transportation has provided a $157 million loan guarantee to COSCO for the building of four ships in Mobile, Alabama. [18]

COSCO is not an altogether unfamiliar name to Clinton-watchers, who have long-noted Clinton's affinity for shady Chinese characters. In 1996 Clinton met with Johnny Chung, a Chinese American businessman who donated $366,000 to the Democrats, money that was later returned for possible illegalities. Chung brought six Chinese officials to the White House to pay their respects to Clinton, and one of the six men was a COSCO advisor. Published reports indicate that it was Clinton who provided materials furnishing details on the leasing of the Long Beach naval base at that meeting.

Clinton also had a coffee klatch with the chairmen of two Chinese guns manufacturing companies. These men were involved in a plot to smuggle 2,000 illegal Chinese weapons into Oakland, California aboard a COSCO vessel. Customs officials have said that there were plans to sell the guns to street gangs. Although the officials who had arranged the shipment of illegal weapons were indicted, COSCO got off scot-free. COSCO has also been implicated in the shipping of illegal aliens into America. [19]

Even as local Long Beach residents were protesting the lease of the naval yard to the Chinese, two truckloads of illegal arms that had been shipped through the port were intercepted by U.S. Customs. The arms cache included thousands of grenade launchers and M-2 carbines, and was perhaps the largest shipment of illegal weapons ever confiscated. Customs did not know who was responsible for shipping the arms, according to a spokesman's statement, although one can speculate that there would have been a strong motive not to implicate COSCO if they were indeed involved. [20]

And then the Chinese Navy came sailing into San Diego. On March 21, 1997 the Chinese Navy made its first visit to the U.S. mainland. The vessels Harbin, Nancang and Zhuhai docked at the North Island Naval Air Station amid great ceremony. Local activists protested the arrival of the Chinese with an airplane towing the message: "U.S. Welcomes China While Tibet Weeps." [21]

Another telling Clinton/Chinese connection is with John Huang, whose connections with the Clintons go as far back as Hillary Clinton's Rose Law firm. The Lippo Bank of Indonesia — a group partly owned by Chinese military intelligence — funneled two million dollars to the Democratic National Convention through Huang, a "former" employee. Clinton also received a 3.5 million dollar loan from the Lippo group's Worthen Bank during his campaign for president, and Lippo also donated $250,000 that ended up in Webster Hubbell's pocket, widely speculated to be hush money in the Whitewater investigation.

Clinton appointed Huang as Deputy Secretary of Commerce, with top secret security clearance granted a month before Huang stopped working for Lippo. No security vetting was required for the top secret clearance.

While working at the Department of Commerce, Huang received twice-weekly CIA briefings — almost 150 of them — on China and the Pacific Rim without ever having received a background check or government clearance. Huang's phone records show that he promptly called Lippo most weeks after the CIA briefing. [22]

John Huang is also implicated in a deal with Entergy Corporation, that had been run by Erskine Bowles, prior to his taking over the role of George Stephanopolis as top White House aide. Huang bought and arranged the shipping of advanced computer equipment, electronics, and telecommunications equipment destined to be used in Chinese missiles. During CIA and defense intelligence briefings President Clinton assured the assembled brass that the equipment was obsolete, supposedly based upon the statements of Pentagon sources. Far from obsolete, the equipment was state of the art. Clinton, however, now does not recall who the Pentagon sources were who told him the equipment was junk. [23]

Huang is alleged to have arranged private White House meetings between foreign business executives and Clinton, for which the executives dropped a cool $450,000 per meeting. Huang also arranged clandestine deals between the Clinton White House and Peking reported to have been worth about $5 billion, shortly after which Clinton pushed through a Most Favored Nation status for Red China. Huang is currently under investigation by the Department of Justice to determine whether he may have served as an "agent of influence" of China. Why Clinton is not receiving the same scrutiny eludes me. [24]

Clinton's Asian money connections run deeper than front men and banking institutions. The *Washington Post* has written that, "Sensitive intelligence information shows that the Chinese embassy on Connecticut Avenue, N.W. here [in Washington, D.C.] was used for planning contributions to the DNC [Democratic National Committee]." [25]

Interesting that our Commander-in-Chief should be so interested in promoting trade privileges and access for the Chinese, since Clinton has benefited from large donations from Asians and Asian-Americans, returning at least two million dollars of questionable cash because of the raised eyebrows of Congress. But apparently there are other reasons for Clinton's love for the Chinese, more than simply personal profit. Former White House aide George Stephanopoulos, speaking on *ABC This Week,* was so forthcoming as to state that Clinton's support of

China "reflected the influence of the Council on Foreign Relations." [26]

Recent events underline the folly of providing top secret clearances to possible Chinese agents, and in opening up free access to America by the Chinese. A high-level Chinese official only recently threatened to H-Bomb Los Angeles.

Chas Freeman, a former U.S. Ambassador to China and Assistant Secretary of Defense, recalls that a Chinese official relayed to him the "advanced state of military planning" by the Chinese and that "preparations for a missile attack on Taiwan, and the target selection to carry it out, have been completed and await a final decision by the Politburo in Beijing."

Freeman also mentioned that "a Chinese official... asserted that China could act militarily against Taiwan without fear of intervention by the United States because American leaders care more about Los Angeles than they do about Taiwan." [27]

Examining the above facts, the nature of the threat awaiting America is plain. America is being run by New World Order acolytes who view the world through rose — make that Red — colored glasses, although there are other political forces in the world who may not share the same vision... or lack of it.

America still has its enemies, and disarmament may mean nuclear annihilation for this country. This was clearly revealed in 1984 by Anatoliy Golitsyn, in his book *New Lies For Old.* Golitsyn had been an influential KGB officer in Russia prior to his defection to the United States, and was well aware of Communist strategic intentions at the highest levels. Golitsyn believed that Western intelligence and politics was thoroughly penetrated by moles. Golitsyn's cause was championed in America by CIA "spymaster" James Jesus Angleton, who believed what the former KGB agent had to say. Angleton's career came to an end over this very matter.

In retrospect, there is much to suggest that Golitsyn and Angleton were correct in their estimation about the deceptive nature of detente and the penetration of American security by Soviet agents. Referring to the liberalization that has since taken place in the former Soviet Union and in the world, Golitsyn wrote five years in advance of the events, taking on the character of a soothsayer. Golitsyn knew what he was talking about, although his message has been almost entirely hidden from the American people and the world.

According to Golitsyn, writing in 1984, the Soviets would engage in a "public relations strategy" to:

1. Ostensibly surrender control of Eastern Europe.

2. Put on a show of liberalization and to encourage democratic movements in the Soviet Union and Eastern Europe. These movements would be covertly controlled by the KGB. Hardline Communists in positions of power would be replaced by KGB-chosen "reformers."

3. Announce that secret police and intelligence agencies were disbanded, while simply re-organizing and renaming them.

4. Permit East and West Germany to reunify.

5. Give the impression that Communism and the Soviet Empire are dead.

6. With the supposed "thaw" in East/West relations, infiltrate thousands of Communist agents into the West.

America, falling for this Eastern PR blitz, would be expected to make the following concessions:

1. America would take over responsibility for much of Soviet debt, and provide large infusions of capital to the "former" Soviets to save their economy.

2. Numbers of American troops in Western Europe would be vastly decreased.

3. The U.S. and its allies would disarm, following the "dismantling" of the Soviet threat, while the Soviets would continue to covertly increase their armaments and military forces.

Given the Eastern Bloc's new stance, Germany would become neutral, leaning toward an alliance with Russia, thereby neutralizing NATO.

After the disarmament of the West, a deadly surprise is in store, Golitsyn warned us. The Chinese-Soviet ideological split, which has been some 30 or more years in duration, is disinformation, according to the former KGB operative. When the West is disarmed, with American and European security thoroughly penetrated by intelligence agents, the Chinese and Russians will suddenly find it in their hearts to reconcile — as they had planned all along. America, lacking defenses of her own, would then be confronted by the greatest military threat in the world. Checkmate. [28]

NOTES:

1. McAlvaney, Donald S., *McAlvaney Intelligence Advisor,* undated information sheet
2. Jasper, William F., "Conspiracy: Where's the Proof?" *The New American,* September 16, 1996
3. Ammerman, Jim, "The Imminent Military Takover of the USA," spoken presentation to the Prophecy Club
4. *Rocky Mountain News,* September 21, 1994
5. *The Chicago Tribune,* November 4, 1993
6. Keegan, Jr., Major General George, quoted in *Deep Black,* by William E. Burrows, Berkley Books, New York, 1986
7. Defense News, February 6-12, 1995
8. Blair, Mike, "Russian Submarines Prowl U.S. Coasts," *The Spotlight,* January 29, 1996; Evans, G. Russell, "America Warned Not to Go to Sleep," *The Spotlight,* April 18, 1994
9. *The Mail Tribune,* Medford, Oregon, June 1996
10. *The Wall Street Journal,* May 26, 1994; Waller, J. Michael. "Russia's Poisonous Secret," Reader's Digest, undated clipping
11. *Orlando Sentinal,* March 28, 1994
12. McAlvany, Donald S., "Beware of the Bear: The Russian Strategy For World Domination," *The McAlvany Intelligence Advisor,* March 1995
13. "Russians cling to dream of nuclear earthquake weapon," London *Sunday Times,* 15 September, 1996
14. *New York Times* magazine, August 27, 1995
15. Blair, Mike, "Red China Upgrades Nuke Forces," *The Spotlight,* July 18, 1994; "China Nukes Aimed at U.S. Rapidly Increasing," Understanding Defense, undated news release
16. "Chinese Firm to Lease Navy Base," Associated Press, March 9, 1997
17. Lindlaw, Scott, "Residents Worry About Security With Chinese

Shippers at Old Base Site," Associated Press, March 13, 1997; "Clinton Impeachment Inquiry Begins," *Patriot Report,* May 1997; "Asian Influence in Congress Spotted," *The Spotlight,* April 14, 1997

18. "Chinese Firm to Lease Navy Base"; Lindlaw; Arnold, Andrew. "Something Stinks in Washington," *The Spotlight,* April 14, 1997

19. "Arms Smuggled Via Calif. Seized"; *The Free American,* April, 1997; "Chinese Firm to Lease Navy Base"; "Clinton Impeachment Inquiry Begins"

20. "Arms Smuggled Via California Seized," National State Sovereignty Coalition, undated news release

21. Fordahl, Matthew, "Chinese Navy makes first U.S. visit," Associated Press, March 22, 1997

22. "Clinton Impeachment Inquiry Begins"; "Roots of Chinagate Go as Far Back as Little Rock in '77," *The Spotlight,* March 31, 1997; Skolnick, Sherman H., "The Red Chinese Secret Police and the Clinton White House," *Conspiracy Nation,* Volume 10, number 48; Duffy, Brian, "The Rise and Fall of John Huang," The *Washington Post,* May 19, 1997

23. "Clinton Impeachment Inquiry Begins"

24. "Clinton Administration and Red China Locked in Lovers' Embrace," *The Spotlight,* April 21, 1997; Duffy

25. *Washington Post,* quote cited in "China's Role in U.S. Policy Probed," *Middle American News,* March 1997

26. Gurudas, "Red China and Other Nations in the U.S. During the New World Order," unpublished essay, 1997

27. "Clinton Impeachment Inquiry Begins"; Denham, Alyn. "China Acquires U.S. Technology for Missiles," Americans for Sane Policies, undated news release; Blair, Mike. "Clinton Rewards Communists Who Supplied Gangs with Machine Guns," *The Spotlight,* March 31, 1997; Arnold, Andrew, "Aliens Flood Country as Clinton Administration Throws Border Open," *The Spotlight,* March 31, 1997; "Chinese Threaten to Destroy Los Angeles," obtained from the Coalition to Defend America

28. Golitsyn, Anatoliy. *New Lies For Old. Dodd, Mead & Co. New York, 1984*

AFTERWORD

RED ALERT

I t is my experience that most persons, reading a book, experience it only as entertainment. This is no doubt because participation in life has, to a good degree, been replaced by pure spectatorism — "the Society of the Spectacle" as the French refer to it.

People may experience strong emotions when they read a book, they may agree with the author, they may mutter agreement under their breath at the good passages, and perhaps even recommend the book to their Uncle Charlie, but ultimately reading is only a spectator sport in most instances.

It is rare that the spectator crosses over to being a participant in the matters about which they are concerned. Mainly, they just sit on their rears and gripe.

The time for television culture and spectating is long past. It is time to assume the role of adults in creating events rather than simply watching them pass by on a television screen, a computer monitor, or in the pages of books.

There is no more time to waste. We can no longer fool ourselves that we are the children of a benevolent Big Brother. The New Deal of Roosevelt has been turned into the "Tandem Thrusts" of Bill and Hillary royally screwing this country.

We are under attack from globalist forces going under the name of the New World Order, whose purpose is to reduce our lot to that of a Third World country, and perhaps eliminate us as a culture altogether. It is time we did something about the end of America.

As far as strategies for restoring what is ours, I could write a book on that topic alone. I wrote a chapter on it in the first book in this series; if necessary, you may refer to that for specifics. But as far as what to do, the answer is less complicated than you might imagine, in fact it is extraordinarily simple:

Do.

Don't just watch. Don't just collect clippings about government atrocity and watch videos about Waco. Do something to effectively counter the forces that enslave us and future generations. Proceed from your own viewpoint and attack, *in a legal and non-violent fashion,* the forces that oppress this country. Speak out.

At this point we are at a pre-revolutionary stage, where government is only selectively crushing protesters who quibble about the New World Order and its victims. Perhaps there is still time for Americans to take back control of the country in a non-violent fashion, and restore our traditional rights and freedoms by restoring the rule of the Constitution, rather than the dictates of the monied elite.

In my opinion, the most effective tool of persons wanting to restore legal government in this country lies, not in bombs or well-greased uzis, but in communication. Not just receiving communication and piling it in big stacks in your bedroom, but mobilizing, putting it out.

The means of communication available to you are limitless and depend only on your imagination. The pen really is mightier than the sword. So are the TV and radio and computer and simply speaking with people on a one-to-one basis. Expose the New World Order and the vampirism that is being inflicted upon America.

Expose the Red Dove of Communism before Peoria becomes an outright gift to the People's Republic. Let people know what is going on and get them to act legally and sanely, without all the macho posturing of some of the persons in this movement are prone to. Make clear to your elected representatives that if they do not wake up to the destruction of America, that you and your friends will work your hearts out to ensure that they are not re-elected.

We must not be naive: This is not a Sylvester Stallone film. This is not Sergeant York. We are not talking about trying to take out a few bad guys at the top with a bird rifle, but countering a system of the enslavement of our total energies and power, and the erosion of our hard-won rights.

One fortunate thing is that the New World Order depends upon the agreement — or at least the ignorance — of the disenfranchised 99% of the population. Communication is the access we have to combat the lies told in the media, and to break the agreement and the ignorance of the population. We may never reach the majority of the people and make them understand what is going on, but we don't need to. We need to alert the nearly-awake ones who matter.

People, befuddled by the impact of the New World Order, starved of relevant information, appeased by booze and drugs and sports and jiggle-TV, need to be shown. They need to be startled from their complacency with the sudden realization that we are being invaded by the New World Order. And then they need to stand up and legally take back their power.

We don't have to wait for an all-embracing patriotic movement or organization to show us the way, for some charismatic character to lead us out of the New World Order wilderness, in order to make things happen. From experience, that messianic leader is probably in the pay of the government, anyway.

Again and again, I urge you to stay legal so that you can live to work another day, and spread this information to the people of the United States and the world. Don't let yourself be suckered into a no-win situation where you're trying to take on the jackboots of the New World Order with a popgun, or by threatening a mass march by the militia on Washington, as one of our leading "patriots" did a few years back. We don't need Rambos to further alienate the public against governmental reform in America — and the truth.

The solution is simple. Use your head. Stay legal. Get the truth out there. Do what it takes to win against the New World Order.

SOURCES

Adventures Unlimited, One Adventure Place, P.O. Box 74, Kempton, Illinois 60946

A-Albionic Consulting and Research, P.O. Box 20273, Ferndale, Michigan 48220

Factsheet Five, P. O. Box 170099, San Francisco, California 94117-0099

Feral House, 1123 Grant Avenue, Venice, California 90297

Flatland, P.O. Box 2420, Fort Bragg, California 95437

IllumiNet Press, P.O. Box 2808, Lilburn, Georgia 30048

The Leading Edge, P.O. Box 7530, Yelm, Washington 98597

Loompanics Unlimited, P.O. Box 1197, Port Townsend, Washington 98368

The McAlvany Intelligence Advisor, P.O. Box 84904, Phoenix, AZ 85071

Media Bypass, P.O. Box 5326, Evansville, Indiana 47716

M.O.M., P.O. Box 1486, Noxon, Montana 59853

Nexus, P.O. Box 177, Kempton, Illinois 60946-0177

Paranoia Magazine, P.O. Box 1041, Providence, Rhode Island, 02901

The Patriot Report, P.O. Box 1148, Sallisaw, Oklahoma 74955

Prevailing Winds, P.O. Box 23511, Santa Barbara, California 93121

The Spotlight, 300 Independence Avenue, SE, Washington, DC 20003

Steamshovel Press, P.O. Box 23715, St. Louis, Missouri 63121

For a copy of our current catalog
write to:

IllumiNet Press
P.O. Box 2808
Lilburn, GA 30048